Introduction to Foreign Exchange Rates

Introduction to Foreign Exchange Rates

Thomas J. O'Brien

First published in 2013 by
Business Expert Press, LLC
222 East 46th Street, New York, NY 10017
www.businessexpertpress.com

ISBN-13: 978-1-60649-736-4 (paperback)
ISBN-13: 978-1-60649-737-1 (e-book)

Business Expert Press Finance and Financial Management collection

Collection ISSN: Forthcoming (print)
Collection ISSN: Forthcoming (electronic)

Cover and interior design by Exeter Premedia Services Private Ltd., Chennai, India

First edition: 2013

10 9 8 7 6 5 4 3 2 1

Printed in the United States of America.

I thank John Griffin, Alain Krapl, Steve Magee, Dev Mishra, and Chris Malone for their helpful comments and discussions.

Abstract

As managers expand their international business operations, they are confronted by the puzzling and vexing world of foreign exchange (FX) rates. This text is designed as a resource that can help managers quickly understand and navigate the FX market. The text may be used as an introductory module in a course in international finance, whether the course is oriented to international markets, international investments, or international corporate finance. The primary intended audience is an applied MBA course aimed at executives, managers, and would-be managers.

After an introduction to FX rates, the text covers the important topic FX rate valuation. It is important for managers to understand when an FX rate is incorrectly valued, as this situation may have a bearing on corporate decisions on strategy, risk management, capital structure, and overseas investments and operations. The text also covers the mechanics of forward FX contracts, and their use in managing the risk of future foreign currency cash flows.

The text includes a case that unifies the ideas. The case company is faced with FX exposure in the revenues from a proposed new foreign customer. The decision maker applies the text material to evaluate whether the FX rate is over-, under-, or correctly valued. The final decisions are whether to expand sales to the foreign market and whether to hedge the FX risk.

Keywords

foreign exchange rates, international parity conditions, purchasing power, interest rates, forward FX contracts, hedging, FX transaction exposure.

Contents

CHAPTER 1

Foreign Exchange Rates

Global growth is essential to many large companies. Managers need to understand the impact of foreign exchange (FX) rates on corporate results and strategic decisions. This chapter introduces some basic "mechanics" of FX rates. The subsequent chapters cover what economic factors drive FX rates.

Foreign Exchange Rates

An FX rate is, simply, the price of one currency in terms of another. An FX rate between U.S. dollars and British pounds can be expressed as either (a) U.S. dollars per British pound or (b) British pounds per U.S. dollar. We use the notation 2 $/£ to mean 2 U.S. dollars ($2) per British pound, or that $2 will buy 1 British pound. Equivalently, we can use the reciprocal, and say that the FX rate is 0.50 £/$, which means 0.50 British pounds (£0.50) per U.S. dollar, or that £0.50 will buy 1 U.S. dollar.

In general, an FX rate expresses the price of the "denominator currency" in terms of the "numerator currency." The numerator currency is called the *pricing currency*, or the *terms currency*. The denominator currency is sometimes called the *base currency*. Always remember that when we use the expression "FX price of such-and-such currency," we are thinking in terms of that currency as the "denominator currency," and we are expressing its price in terms of the "numerator currency." For 2 $/£, we are expressing the FX price of the British pound in terms of the U.S. dollar as the pricing currency. For 0.50 £/$, we are expressing the FX price of the U.S. dollar in terms of the British pound as the pricing currency.

In financial markets, FX rate quotes usually involve the U.S. dollar as one of the two currencies. The usual convention is to quote the FX rate with the U.S. dollar as the base currency. For example, an FX quote of 1.20 in the case of the Swiss franc (the "Swissie") implies 1.20 Swiss francs per U.S. dollar, or

1.20 Sf/$, and an FX quote of 108 for the Japanese yen means 108 yen per U.S. dollar, or 108 ¥/$. The common FX market convention to quote the FX price of the U.S. dollar is called *European terms,* although the pricing currency involved is not necessarily a European currency. The convention to quote most FX rates in European terms emerged after World War II, when the U.S. dollar replaced the British pound as the principal international currency. Basically, the FX rates expressed the price of 1 U.S. dollar in terms of the currency of each country, many of which were European.

Although most FX rates are conventionally quoted in European terms, a few important currencies are typically quoted with the U.S. dollar as the pricing currency. This style is referred to as *American terms.* An FX quote of 1.50 in the case of the British pound means 1.50 U.S. dollars per British pound, or 1.50 $/£, which is the FX price of a British pound (in U.S. dollars). Other significant currencies usually quoted in American terms include the Australian dollar (A$) and the New Zealand dollar (NZ$). Before World War II, the tradition was to quote FX rates as the FX price of one British pound in terms of the other currency, because the British pound was the main international currency. Even after the U.S. dollar replaced the British pound as the main international currency, the traditional quotation style was retained for the British pound and currencies of some countries of the former British Empire.

When the euro (€) emerged in the 1990s as the common currency of many European countries, the American terms convention was adopted for the important FX rate between euros and U.S. dollars. For example, a quote of 1.35 for the euro means 1.35 U.S. dollars per euro, or 1.35 $/€, which is the FX price of one euro in terms of U.S. dollars. The euro is the currency of 17 of the 27 countries of the *European Union.* The 17 countries using the euro are known collectively as the *Eurozone:* Austria, Belgium, Cyprus, Estonia, Finland, France, Germany, Greece, Ireland, Italy, Luxembourg, Malta, the Netherlands, Portugal, Slovakia, Slovenia, and Spain. Of the 10 EU member countries outside the Eurozone, seven are obligated to join once they fulfill the strict entrance requirements: Bulgaria, the Czech Republic, Hungary, Latvia, Lithuania, Poland, and Romania. Three EU member countries are not obligated to join the Eurozone and have their own currencies: Sweden, Denmark, and the United Kingdom. Switzerland is not in the EU.

The FX rates seen streaming on Bloomberg TV and CNBC follow the market's quotation conventions, as does this text. So you should try to get used to them. For major currencies, it will help to remember that the euro, the British pound, the Australian dollar, and the New Zealand dollar are typically quoted in American terms, while all the rest are usually in European terms.

An FX rate for immediate delivery is called a *spot FX rate*. The notation for a spot FX rate in this text is the capital letter X. To keep things straight, generally we'll follow X with a two-currency superscript. Thus, $X^{SF/\$}$ represents a spot FX rate expressed in Swiss francs per U.S. dollar, which is in conventional European terms of the FX price of the U.S. dollar (in Swiss francs). $X^{\$/\pounds}$ would represent a spot FX rate expressed in U.S. dollars per British pound, which is the American terms convention for the FX price of the pound (in U.S. dollars). We'll often use a subscript to denote time, in years from the present. Thus $X_0^{\$/\pounds}$ denotes a current spot FX rate, $X_2^{\$/\pounds}$ a spot FX rate two years from now, $X_{0.50}^{\$/\pounds}$ a spot FX rate six months from now, and so forth.

Exhibit 1.1 shows some representative spot FX rates, as conventionally quoted, for some recent times.

Exhibit 1.1. Selected Spot FX Rates

	May 1, 08	Jan 26, 09	Mar 15, 13
Australian dollar (AUD*)	0.934	0.654	1.04
Brazilian real (BRL)	1.66	2.40	1.98
Canadian dollar (CAD)	1.02	1.23	1.02
Swiss franc (CHF)	1.05	1.15	0.94
Chinese yuan (CHN)	6.99	6.85	6.22
Euro (EUR*)	1.55	1.30	1.31
British pound (GBP*)	1.95	1.38	1.51
Indian rupee (IRP)	40.6	49.7	37.2
Japanese yen (JPY)	104	89	95
Korean won (KRW)	1.004	1.379	1.111
New Zealand dollar (NZD*)	0.78	0.51	0.83

*Quoted in American terms; all others in European terms.
Source: *Yahoo* finance.

From a country's perspective, an FX rate is said to be in *direct terms* if the home currency is the pricing currency and in *indirect terms* if the foreign currency is the pricing currency. Thus, the FX rate of 2 $/£ is in direct terms from the U.S. point of view, because the U.S. dollar is the pricing currency, that is, in the numerator. The FX rate of 0.50 £/$ is in *indirect terms* from the U.S. point of view, but is in direct terms from the British point of view.

The FX rate for the Swiss franc is 1.25 Sf/$.

(a) What is the FX price of the Swiss franc (in U.S. dollars)?

(b) What is the FX price of the U.S. dollar (in Swiss francs)?

(c) The FX rate quote is in direct terms from the point of view of Switzerland: True or False?

(d) The FX rate is in American terms: True or False?

(e) The Swiss franc is the pricing currency: True or False?

(f) The Swiss franc is the base currency: True or False?

Answers: (a) 0.80 $/Sf; (b) 1.25 Sf/$; (c) True; (d) False; (e) True; (e) False.

The FX rate for the euro is 1.60 $/€.

(a) What is the FX price of the euro (in U.S. dollars)?

(b) What is the FX price of the U.S. dollar (in euros)?

(c) The FX rate quote is in direct terms from the point of view of the Eurozone: True or False?

(d) The FX rate is in American terms: True or False?

(e) The euro is the pricing currency: True or False?

(f) The euro is the terms currency: True or False?

Answers: (a) 1.60 $/€; (b) 0.625 €/$; (c) False; (d) True; (e) False; (f) False.

In 2010, spot FX market transactions accounted for 37% of the $4 trillion of average daily total FX market turnover. The other categories of FX market transactions, which we'll go into later, are FX forwards, currency swaps, FX swaps, and options. Exhibit 1.2 shows some total FX market turnover trends by currency.

Exhibit 1.2. Currency Distribution of Total FX Market Turnover
(Percentage shares of average daily turnover; total = 200%)

	2001	2004	2007	2010
U.S. dollar	89.9	88.0	85.6	84.9
Euro	37.9	37.4	37.0	39.1
Japanese yen	23.5	20.8	17.2	19.0
Pound sterling	13.0	16.5	14.9	12.9
Australian dollar	4.3	6.0	6.6	7.6
Swiss franc	6.0	6.0	6.8	6.4
Canadian dollar	4.5	4.2	4.3	5.3
Swedish krona	2.5	2.2	2.7	2.2
Hong Kong dollar	2.2	1.8	2.7	2.4

Source: Bank for International Settlements.

Flexible Versus Fixed FX Rates

Currencies differ with regard to the degree to which supply and demand in the FX market is allowed to determine the FX rate. At one extreme, the FX rate is determined entirely by private market supply and demand. This type of FX rate is called a *flexible FX rate* or a *floating FX rate*. At the other extreme is a fixed FX rate, determined by government policy. In actual practice, a flexible FX rate, such as the FX rate between U.S. dollars and euros, is only mostly determined by private markets, and is sometimes also subject to *some* government policy influence. And a fixed FX rate, such as the one between U.S. dollars and Chinese yuan, may be allowed to change from time to time and hence is not perfectly fixed. There are also many instances of intermediate situations where the FX rate is partially flexible and partially fixed.

As we said, sometimes central banks in flexible FX rate regimes try to affect FX rates to implement economic policy goals. One approach is to initiate transactions in the FX market that are large enough in size to have an influence on the FX rate. This activity is termed *direct intervention*. The U.S. Treasury and Federal Reserve each have independent legal authority to directly intervene in the FX market. In early 2004, a significant direct intervention was conducted by the Bank of Japan, buying U.S. dollars with Japanese yen to reduce the FX price of the yen. Sometimes, several central banks act in a coordinated manner to influence FX rates to achieve some multilateral policy goals reached by negotiation and compromise. In addition to direct intervention in the FX market, we will see later how central banks may influence FX rates through interest rate policy.

Flexible FX rate regimes are typical of advanced economies. In many cases of advanced economies, the actions by central banks may cause FX rates to differ from levels other than what the free market would establish, but central banks do not exert enough power to rigidly control FX rates, even when several central banks act in coordination. In fact, the trading volume of central banks as a whole is small relative to the overall currency market. Central banks are simply market participants, albeit major ones, in the essentially unregulated interbank FX market.

Economies not classified as advanced are either (a) emerging or (b) developing, with the emerging economies being stronger than developing economies. Exhibit 1.3 shows countries that are classified as advanced and emerging in a report of the International Monetary Fund (IMF). Not listed in Exhibit 1.3 are 93 countries classified as developing. The governments of emerging and developing economies tend to exert more influence over the FX rate involving the country's currency.

Exhibit 1.3. Advanced and Emerging Economies

Advanced
Australia, Canada, Hong Kong, Iceland, Israel, Japan, New Zealand, Singapore, Switzerland, and United States *Non-Eurozone EU members*: Denmark, Sweden, and United Kingdom All Eurozone members, except Estonia, Malta, and Slovenia

Emerging
Asia: China, India, Indonesia, Korea, Malaysia, Pakistan, Philippines, Russia, Sri Lanka, Thailand, Ukraine *Latin America*: Argentina, Brazil, Chile, Colombia, Dominican Republic, Ecuador, El Salvador, Mexico, Panama, Peru, Uruguay, Venezuela *Europe*: Bulgaria, Czech Republic, Hungary, Poland, Slovak Republic *Middle East*: Egypt, Jordan, Oman, Saudi Arabia, Turkey *Africa*: Côte d'Ivoire, Morocco, Nigeria, South Africa, Tunisia, Zimbabwe

Source: The empirics of exchange rate regimes and trade: Words vs. Deeds, Mahvash Saeed Qureshi and Charalambos Tsangarides, *IMF working paper*, February 2010.

Figure 1.1 depicts the distribution of FX rate regimes (flexible, intermediate, and fixed) across classifications of economies (advanced, emerging, and developing). The left-hand diagrams are the "de jure" FX rate regimes, or the FX rate regime announced by the economy. The right-hand diagrams are the "de facto" FX rate regimes, or the FX rate regime based on actual events and policies.

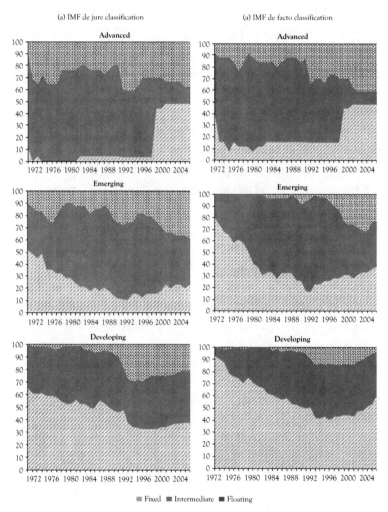

Figure 1.1. Exchange rate regimes, 1972–2006.

Source: The empirics of exchange rate regimes and trade: Words vs. Deeds, Mahvash Saeed Qureshi and Charalambos Tsangarides, *IMF working paper*, February 2010.

At the present time, the Chinese government controls the FX rate between Chinese yuan and U.S. dollars by not allowing the convertibility of the yuan for portfolio flows. That is, banks and other investors outside of China may not hold balances and securities denominated in yuan. The cost of Chinese trade products is affected by the spot FX rate fixed by the Chinese government. Chinese exporters, when paid in U.S. dollars, exchange the U.S. dollars for yuan with internal Chinese banks at the official spot FX rate. The basic idea is depicted in Figure 1.2. Over time, the Chinese government has occasionally changed the official FX rate, typically raising the FX price of the yuan in terms of U.S. dollars.

Sometimes the central bank of an emerging or developing economy tries to control the FX price of its currency too rigidly. If the currency is freely convertible, this can lead to a currency crisis. Sometimes a government of an emerging or developing country restricts the convertibility of its currency and dictates an *official FX rate*. If this happens, a free market for the currency may spring up. If the government tolerates this free market, it is called a *parallel market*. If not, it is called a *black market*.

Appreciation/Depreciation of a Currency

If the FX rate for yen goes from 125 ¥/$ to 160 ¥/$, this change is an appreciation of the U.S. dollar relative to the yen. We also infer that the yen has depreciated, because the change implies that the FX price of the yen (in terms of the U.S. dollar) has dropped from 0.008 $/¥ to 0.00625 $/¥.

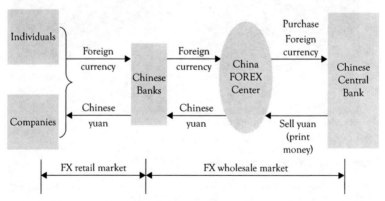

Figure 1.2. Currency exchange in China.

In the press, you will often see confusing announcements like "the yen fell from 118 ¥/$ to 120 ¥/$" or "the U.S. dollar rose from 1.43 $/€ to 1.38 $/€". Just remember that because the euro depreciates when the FX rate goes from 1.43 $/€ to 1.38 $/€, the U.S. dollar appreciates. So it is not incorrect to say that "the U.S. dollar rose from 1.43 $/€ to 1.38 $/€"—just a little confusing at first. Thinking of an FX rate as being the FX price of the "denominator" currency helps out if you are new to this subject.

If the spot FX rate for the Swiss franc drops from 1.50 Sf/$ to 1.20 Sf/$, has the Swiss franc depreciated against the U.S. dollar? If the FX rate for the euro drops from 1.50 $/€ to 1.20 $/€, has the U.S. dollar depreciated against the euro?

Answers: No to both. The Swiss franc has appreciated. Since 1 U.S. dollar will buy fewer Swiss francs at 1.20 Sf/$, the FX price of the U.S. dollar has depreciated and the Swiss franc has appreciated. In the second question, the FX price of the U.S. dollar has appreciated and the euro has depreciated.

Figures 1.3–1.5 depict the historical movement of three important spot FX rates: $/€, ¥/$, and Sf/$.

Some reports on FX rates use the terms *devaluation* instead of depreciation and *revaluation* instead of appreciation. Devaluation has the same

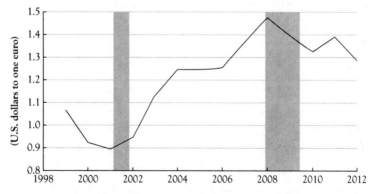

Figure 1.3. U.S./Euro foreign exchange rate.

Note: Shaded areas indicate U.S. recessions. 2013 research.stlouisfed.org
Source: Board of governors of the Federal Reserve system

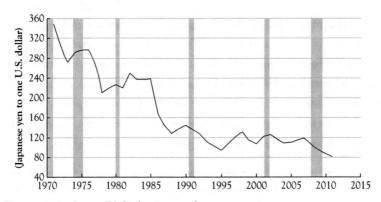

Figure 1.4. Japan/U.S. foreign exchange rate.

Note: Shaded areas indicate U.S. recessions. 2013 research.stlouisfed.org
Source: Board of governors of the Federal Reserve system

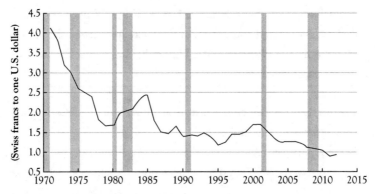

Figure 1.5. Switzerland/U.S. foreign exchange rate.

Note: Shaded areas indicate U.S. recessions. 2013 research.stlouisfed.org
Source: Board of governors of the Federal Reserve system

result on an FX rate as depreciation, and revaluation has the same result as appreciation. The difference is that devaluation and revaluation refer to a change in an FX rate caused by government policy, whereas the terms depreciation and appreciation imply FX rate changes caused by other market forces. If a central bank intervenes, or even several central banks in a coordinated effort intervene, in the currency market to try to influence the FX price of a currency, this action represents official policy, and the terms devaluation and revaluation would be applicable.

Cross-Rates

A *cross-rate* is an FX rate between two non-U.S. dollar currencies. A *cross-market* is a market for direct transactions between non-U.S. dollar currencies. If one wants to change euros into yen, for example, one may do so directly in that cross-market. An interbank cross-market exists for euros/Swiss francs; euros/British pounds; euros/Japanese yen; and British pounds/Japanese yen.

In the absence of a cross-market, the U.S. dollar serves as a *vehicle currency*, meaning that to exchange one non-U.S. dollar currency for another involves two trades, first to exchange one currency into U.S. dollars and then to exchange the U.S. dollars into the second currency. In Exhibit 1.2 you can see that in 2010, the U.S. dollar was involved in roughly 85% of FX trades. This statistic seems to imply that roughly 15% of FX trades in 2010 were direct cross-market trades.

If the spot FX rate for euros and U.S. dollars is 1.20 $/€ and the Swiss franc trades at 1.00 Sf/$, it stands to reason that the cross-rate for euros and Swiss francs should be (1.20 $/€)(1.00 Sf/$) = 1.20 Sf/€, or 0.8333 €/Sf. If the actual cross-rate is not equal to 1.20 Sf/€, a trading activity called triangular arbitrage may be used to make "easy money." This trading activity will tend to drive the actual cross-rate into alignment with the other two FX rates. The next section, Triangular Arbitrage, describes this process. (Readers who do not want this detail should skip the section.)

The spot FX rates are 1.60 $/£ and 1.20 $/€.

(a) What should the cross-rate be for British pounds and euros, in direct terms from the British perspective?

(b) If the euro depreciates by 25% relative to the U.S. dollar, but the euro/pound cross-rate does not change, what is the percentage change in the FX price of the British pound (in U.S. dollars)?

Answers: (a) The cross-rate for euros and pounds should be (1.20 $/€)/(1.60 $/£) = 0.75 £/€. (b) If the euro depreciates relative to the U.S. dollar by 25%, to 0.90 $/€, but the euro/pound FX rate does not change, it must be the case that the pound also depreciates relative to the U.S. dollar to (0.90 $/€)/(0.75 £/€) = 1.20 $/£, which is a 25% depreciation of the pound.

The last example demonstrates a unilateral appreciation of the U.S. dollar relative to the other currencies, perhaps driven by some economic development in the United States. The next example demonstrates a unilateral depreciation of the euro relative to the other currencies, driven perhaps by some economic development in the Eurozone.

Given FX rates of 1.60 $/£ and 1.20 $/€, the British pound/euro FX cross-rate must be 0.75 £/€. If the euro depreciates by 25% relative to the U.S. dollar, but the U.S. dollar/pound FX rate does not change, what must the new pound/euro FX cross-rate be?

Answer: (0.90 $/€)/(1.60 $/£) = 0.5625 £/€, which is a 25% depreciation of the euro relative to the pound.

Triangular Arbitrage

Arbitrage is defined as the simultaneous purchase and sale of essentially the same good or security at different prices. When a cross-market exists and the direct cross-rate is different from the indirect, derived cross-rate, *triangular arbitrage* is theoretically possible. For example, assume the cross-market's direct FX rate for euros/Swiss francs is 0.80 €/Sf at the same time that the euro trades at 1.20 $/€ and the Swiss franc trades at 1.00 Sf/$. The indirect cross-rate in Sf/€ is (1.20 $/€)(1.00 Sf/$) = 1.20 Sf/€, or 0.8333 €/Sf. In this case, triangular arbitrage is possible because 0.80 €/Sf ≠ 0.8333 €/Sf.

To think about how to capture the arbitrage profit, note that the FX price of the Swiss franc, in euros, is lower in the direct cross-market than in the indirect market where the U.S. dollar is as a vehicle. Thus, remembering to "buy low and sell high," you should buy Swiss francs with euros directly (at 0.80 €/Sf) and simultaneously sell Swiss francs for euros indirectly (at 0.8333 €/Sf) using the U.S. dollar vehicle. Selling Swiss francs for euros indirectly means selling Swiss francs for U.S. dollars and then selling the U.S. dollars for euros. For example, you take 0.80 euros to buy 1 Swiss franc directly; sell the 1 Swiss franc for U.S. dollars to get $1; and then use $1 to buy euros at 1.20 $/€, to get $1/(1.20 $/€) = €0.8333. You start with €0.80 and end up with €0.8333, for an arbitrage profit of €0.0333.

Maybe this arbitrage will be easier to see if you start with U.S. dollars. The key is that you want to take advantage of a mispricing and buy Swiss francs with euros directly. So the first step is to exchange the U.S. dollars into euros. Say you start with $1.20 million and you exchange this amount into €1 million. With €1 million, you directly buy Swiss francs: (€1 million)/(0.80 €/Sf) = Sf 1.25 million. With Sf 1.25 million, you buy (Sf 1.25 million)/(1 Sf/$) = $1.25 million. Your arbitrage profit from these hypothetical transactions is $50,000. Figure 1.6 depicts this strategy.

The potential for triangular arbitrage will tend to enforce the alignment of direct cross-rates with derived cross-rates. In the previous euro/ Swiss franc example, the direct purchase of Swiss francs with euros in the cross-market will, other things equal, cause the FX price of the Swiss franc (in euros) to appreciate to higher than 0.80 €/Sf. By the same token, the sale of Swiss francs for U.S. dollars and the purchase of euros with U.S. dollars in the indirect vehicle approach will tend to drive down the FX price of the Swiss franc in U.S. dollars and drive up the FX price of the euros in U.S. dollars. This activity results in a lower derived cross-market FX price of the Swiss franc (in euros) than 0.8333 €/Sf. Arbitrage activity is likely to continue until the direct cross-rate and the derived cross-rate have converged, at which point no further arbitrage is possible. In reality, the potential for profits from triangular arbitrage results in the situation where not such profits are possible.

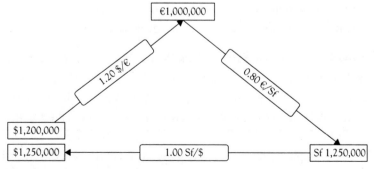

Figure 1.6. *Triangular arbitrage.*

Exhibit 1.4. Yahoo FX Quotes, November 15, 2003

	¥/$	¥/Sf	Sf/$
Bid	108.00	81.3862	1.3267
Ask	108.12	81.4954	1.3273

In reality, triangular arbitrage should consider trading costs. Exhibit 1.4 shows some bid-ask FX rates reported on *Yahoo* on November 15, 2003. At a bid rate, you can buy the numerator currency with the denominator currency. At an ask rate, you can buy the denominator currency with the numerator currency.

Bid: The price at which the numerator currency may be purchased with the denominator currency.

Ask: The price at which the denominator currency may be purchased with the numerator currency.

We can show that there are no triangular arbitrage opportunities in the real-world quotes in Exhibit 1.4. Let us say that you start with $1 million. You first buy Sf 1.3267 million. With the Sf 1.3267 million, you then buy yen, (81.3862 ¥/Sf)(Sf 1.3267 million) = ¥107.975 million. With ¥107.975 million, you buy U.S. dollars, obtaining (¥107.975 million)/ (108.12 ¥/$) = $998,660. You lose $1 million − 998,660 = $1,340 with these transactions. This scenario is depicted in Figure 1.7. The next example demonstrates that you would also lose money by going the other route of first buying yen, then Swiss francs, and finally U.S. dollars.

Start with $1 million. Use the bid–ask quotes in Exhibit 1.4 to buy yen, then buy Swiss francs, then buy U.S. dollars. What is your loss?

Answer: You first buy ¥108 million. With this amount, you next buy (¥108 million)/(81.4954 ¥/Sf) = Sf 1.3252 million. Buying U.S. dollars with Sf 1.3252 million, you buy (Sf 1.3252 million)/ (1.3273 Sf/$) = $998,418. Your loss is $1 million − 998,418 = $1,582.

The examples with the FX rate quotes in Exhibit 1.4 show that triangular arbitrage opportunities do not generally exist in the real world

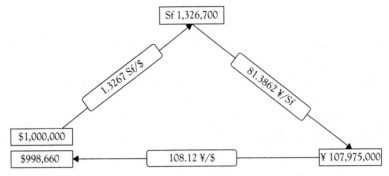

Figure 1.7. Absence of triangular arbitrage.

when bid–ask spreads are considered. In the real world, only professional FX traders would have access to the small triangular arbitrage opportunities that temporarily occur. The buying and selling by professional traders pressures the opportunities away as the professionals capture the profits.

Summary Action Points

- An FX expresses the price of the "denominator" currency in terms of the "numerator" currency. The $/€ FX rate is the FX price of the euro in terms of the U.S. dollar, and the ¥/$ FX rate in FX price of the U.S. dollar in terms of yen.
- An increase in the $/€ FX rate is an appreciation of the euro against the U.S. dollar and a depreciation of the U.S. dollar against the euro. A decrease in the ¥/$ FX rate is an appreciation of the yen against the U.S. dollar and a depreciation of the U.S. dollar against the yen.
- Governments of less-developed countries tend to exert more control over the country's currency than do more developed economies.
- Given the Sf/$ and ¥/$ FX rates, there is an implied FX cross-rate between Swiss francs and yen. If the actual FX cross-rate differs from the indirect FX cross-rate, an arbitrage profit is possible in principle. But since many currency traders are constantly searching for such arbitrage possibilities, the FX rates stay very well aligned.

Glossary

American terms: An FX rate quotation expressed as U.S. dollars per one unit of another currency.

Arbitrage: The simultaneous purchase and sale of essentially the same good or security at different prices.

Base currency: An expression sometimes used to refer to the "denominator" currency in an FX rate.

Black market: Illegal trading of a currency that has an official FX rate dictated by the country's government.

Cross-market: A market for direct exchange of two non-U.S. dollar currencies.

Cross-rate: An FX rate between two non-U.S. dollar currencies.

Devaluation: A drop in a currency's FX price brought about by official policy.

Direct intervention: The purchase and sale of currencies by central banks to influence FX rates.

Direct terms: An FX rate expressed as the amount of one's home currency price per one unit of a foreign currency.

European terms: An FX rate quotation expressed as the number of units of a currency per 1 U.S. dollar.

Flexible (floating) FX rates: FX rates determined by market forces, as opposed to fixed, or pegged, FX rates.

Foreign exchange rate: The price of one currency in terms of another.

Indirect terms: An FX rate expressed as the amount of foreign currency per one unit of one's base currency price.

Official FX rate: An FX rate sometimes dictated by the government of a less-developed country whose currency is not freely convertible.

Parallel market: Trading in a currency that is tolerated by a government that has dictated an official FX rate.

Pricing currency: The "numerator" currency in an FX rate that expresses the price of another currency. Also called the *terms currency*.

Revaluation: An increase in the FX price of a currency brought about by official policy.

Spot FX rate: Exchange rate for immediate delivery.

Terms currency: The "numerator" currency in an FX rate that expresses the price of another currency. Also called the *pricing currency*.

Triangular arbitrage: The strategy to exploit the difference between a direct cross-rate and a derived cross-rate.

Discussion Questions

1. Explain how China is able to stabilize the spot FX rate between the yuan and U.S. dollars.
2. Are you likely to be able to conduct triangular arbitrage? Explain.

Problems

1. The spot FX rate between U.S. dollars and British pounds is 1.60 $/£.
   (a) What is the FX price of the pound?
   (b) What is the FX price of the U.S. dollar?
   (c) The spot FX rate quote is in direct terms from the point of view of the United States: True or False?
   (d) The spot FX rate is in European terms: True or False?
   (e) The pound is the pricing currency: True or False?
2. The spot FX rate for the Swiss franc is 0.80 Sf/$.
   (a) What is the FX price of the Swiss franc?
   (b) What is the FX price of the U.S. dollar?
3. If the spot FX rate for the Japanese yen changes from 80 ¥/$ to 90 ¥/$, has the U.S. dollar (a) appreciated or (b) depreciated against the yen?
4. (a) If the spot FX rate for the Japanese yen changes from 120 ¥/$ to 90 ¥/$, has the yen appreciated or depreciated against the U.S. dollar?
   (b) If the spot FX rate for the British pound changes from 1.50 $/£ to 1.80 $/£, has the U.S. dollar appreciated or depreciated against the pound?
5. Assume there is a direct cross-market for British pounds/Swiss francs. Assume the spot FX rates with the U.S. dollar are 1.50 Sf/$ and 1.50 $/£. What should the direct cross-rate be for Sf/£?
6. Use the information in the previous question. If the direct cross-rate is 2.50 Sf/£, describe the triangular arbitrage strategy.

Answers to Problems

1. (a) 1.60 $/£; (b) 0.625 £/$; (c) True; (d) False; (e) False.
2. (a) 1.25 $/Sf; (b) 0.80 Sf/$.

3. (a) Appreciated against the yen.
4. (a) The yen appreciated. Because 1 U.S. dollar will buy fewer yen at 90 ¥/$, the U.S. dollar depreciated and the yen has appreciated.
   (b) The U.S. dollar depreciated and the pound appreciated.
5. The direct Swiss franc–British pound cross-rate should be 2.25 Sf/£.
6. To execute a "buy-low/sell high" strategy, you first buy pounds with Swiss francs "low" at 2.25 Sf/£ indirectly (by buying U.S. dollars first). Then sell pounds "high" at 2.50 Sf/£ directly into Swiss francs. Starting with U.S. dollars ($1.50), you buy pounds (£1) with U.S. dollars to sell pounds "high" directly into Swiss francs (Sf 2.50); sell the Sf 2.50 back into U.S. dollars at 1.50 Sf/$ to get (Sf 2.50)/(1.50 Sf/$) = $1.67. Profit = $0.17.

CHAPTER 2

Foreign Exchange Volatility

Although spot foreign exchange (FX) rates at the moment are known and observable, one does not know ahead of time what the path of any future spot FX rate will be. Many try to predict and speculate, but there is always uncertainty about where FX rates will go in the future. Some FX rates are more volatile than others, depending on supply and demand and whether government policies tend to stabilize or destabilize. In this chapter, we explain some of the supply and demand factors that affect FX rates, and some of the workings of the market for FX rates. We go into the reasons why FX rates can be volatile like stock prices, and why this volatility creates problems for companies.

Fundamental Supply and Demand for FX

International trade and investing generate supply and demand for FX transactions. To see an example of an FX transaction in international trade, assume that Belmont Manufacturing in the United States imports components from Crown Materials Ltd. in England. Naturally, Belmont's home currency is the U.S. dollar, whereas Crown's home currency is the British pound. Belmont and Crown must agree on the currency in which the payment is to be made. If Crown requires payment in pounds, Belmont must first buy the pounds from a bank in exchange for U.S. dollars. If Belmont is permitted to send payment in U.S. dollars, Crown will exchange those funds with a bank for pounds. In either payment case, there is a *retail FX transaction* between a commercial currency user and a bank. Crown's ultimate need for pounds, to pay employees and other expenses, means a demand in the FX market for pounds and a supply of U.S. dollars.

Retail FX demand originates from other sources besides import/export trade. One example is *foreign direct investment (FDI)* of capital into overseas plant and equipment. A German company wishing to build or buy a plant in Canada needs to exchange euros into Canadian dollars, that is, buy Canadian dollars with euros, to make the investment.

Another source of retail FX demand is *portfolio investment*, which applies to financial securities, rather than FDI in the form of physical capital. (Technically, the purchase of more than 10% of a company's equity by a foreign investor is classified as FDI rather than portfolio investment.) A Hong Kong bond portfolio manager wishing to invest in Japanese bonds needs to exchange Hong Kong dollars into yen to buy the bonds. Upon the liquidation of the bonds, the manager presumably sells the yen back into Hong Kong dollars. A U.S. company might borrow by selling yen-denominated bonds and FX the proceeds into U.S. dollars to fund U.S. dollar assets.

Taken together, international trade, FDI, and portfolio investments are fundamental sources of supply and demand for FX transactions. In 2001, the daily volume of FX transactions for portfolio trades was $329 billion, while the volume of FX transactions by corporate entities for international trade and FDI was a combined $156 billion. Between 1998 and 2001, the volume of FX trading by corporate entities dropped, as firms' treasury departments became more efficient in netting a company's FX trading internally. By contrast, the volume of FX transactions for portfolio investments rose as international portfolio diversification increased.

Another source of demand for some currencies is as a store of value. In general, nations whose economic policies have promoted economic growth and stability, and controlled inflation, will tend to have currencies that appreciate in price over currencies of countries with the opposite policies. The currencies of wealthy, low inflation, growth-oriented economies are referred to as *hard currencies*, and the currencies of the weaker, high-inflation economies are referred to as *soft currencies*. There is an additional demand for hard currencies as a basic store of value for individuals, corporations, and governments in soft-currency countries, especially during financial crises. The U.S. dollar, the Swiss franc, and the euro are the currencies in the highest demand for this purpose.

Interbank FX Market

In either of the possible FX transactions in the Belmont/Crown scenario, a bank provides a retail customer with British pounds in return for U.S.

dollars. Unless the bank has an inventory of pounds, the bank itself needs to acquire the pounds for U.S. dollars. One candidate is the country's central bank, which is the Federal Reserve (the Fed) for a U.S. bank or the Bank of England for a U.K. bank. Another candidate is another bank anywhere in the world.

Transactions between relatively large banks are said to take place in the wholesale *interbank (FX) market.* A small regional bank without direct trading access to the global interbank market may obtain currency from one of the larger interbank participants, possibly through one of a number of established FX brokers. An *FX broker* buys currency in the interbank market and, in turn, sells the currency at a markup to smaller players.

The interbank FX market operates globally, allowing a large number of banks and FX brokers of different nationalities to routinely exchange currencies with each other, with large corporations, and with large fund managers. The need for FX transactions is immense and the vast interbank market has well over $1 trillion worth of trades daily. Wholesale interbank FX trading between interbank dealers was approximately $689 billion in 2001. In the interbank market, no physical paper (banknotes or drafts) changes hands. All transactions take place electronically through an international clearing system. Generally, the FX market is unregulated.

Central Banks and Balance of Payments

In addition to retail and interbank elements, central bank are important FX market participants. A central bank has an unlimited supply of its own economy's currency. In addition, a central bank will maintain balances of *foreign currency reserves (or FX reserves)* of other currencies, obtained over time through transactions in the interbank market. In their FX reserves, central banks like to hold currencies that hold value. In 2012, the most prominent reserve currencies were (1) the U.S. dollar (62%), (2) the euro (25%), (3) the British pound (4%), and (4) the Japanese yen (4%).

To see an example of routine interaction between central banks and the private FX market, say the Bank of England has sold British pounds to Crown Materials' U.S. bank for the U.S. dollars sent to Crown by Belmont. The Bank of England can either hold the U.S. dollars as FX reserves, or trade the U.S. dollars back to the Fed for some of the Fed's existing FX reserves of British pounds (or for gold or other currency). If Belmont had acquired British pounds from its U.S. bank, which in turn had acquired the pounds from the Fed, the Fed would then be holding fewer British pounds in its FX reserves. If the Fed thinks the new inventory level of British pounds is too low, the Fed can buy more pounds in the interbank market, or from the Bank of England using gold or U.S. dollars or, for that matter, any other country's currency that the Fed is holding as FX reserves. If either of the central banks is in the transaction, then there is an increase in the British pound *money supply*, that is, pounds circulating outside the central banking system, and a decline in the money supply of U.S. dollars circulating outside the central bank system.

Whenever a country has a net outflow of currency (including gold), the country has a *balance of payments (BOP) deficit*. A BOP deficit means that the country's total purchases of foreign goods plus its investments into foreign assets exceed the total purchases of the country's goods by foreigners plus investments by foreigners in the country's assets. The result of a BOP deficit is a reduction in the *net FX reserves* held by the country's central bank. The opposite is a *BOP surplus*, with a corresponding gain of net FX reserves. If, over a given period, the value of all U.S. purchases of British goods and investments is less than the value of British purchases of U.S. goods and investments, the United States has a BOP surplus versus the United Kingdom, and the United Kingdom has a BOP deficit versus its trading partner. These ideas are depicted in Figure 2.1.

Figure 2.1 shows a BOP surplus for the United States and a deficit for the United Kingdom. Britain's total of imports of goods from the United States and investments into the United States exceeds the U.S. total of

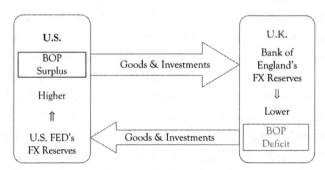

Figure 2.1. Cross-border flows, balance of payments, and FX reserves.

imports from the United Kingdom and investments into the United Kingdom. The FX reserves held by the U.S. Federal Reserve rise, and those held by the Bank of England drop.

The United States increases imports from Switzerland. Other things the same, the net FX reserves held by the Fed will (a) rise, or (b) drop. Choose (a) or (b).

Answer: (b) Net FX reserves of the U.S. Fed will drop.

Portfolio managers in the United States increase investment into Canadian securities. Other things the same, the net FX reserves held by the Fed will (a) rise, or (b) drop. Choose (a) or (b).

Answer: (b) Net FX reserves of the U.S. Fed will drop.

China runs a large BOP surplus versus the United States, accumulating large balance of FX reserves of U.S. dollars. Of course, these reserves cannot be used to buy yuan in the interbank FX market, because no yuan balances are held outside of China. Instead, China's large balances of U.S. dollars are mainly used to buy and hold interest-bearing U.S. Treasury securities.

Fundamental supply and demand tends to drive FX rate changes in a flexible FX rate regime in the following way: Suppose that owing to a net Japanese purchase of U.S. investments, yen are currently being sold for U.S. dollars, that is, yen are being used to buy U.S. dollars. Then the buying pressure on the U.S. dollar causes the FX price of the U.S. dollar to rise. Alternatively, we can say that the FX price of the yen decreases in terms of the U.S. dollar because of the selling of yen. If instead there is buying pressure on the yen, the FX price of the yen rises relative to the U.S. dollar (and the FX price of the U.S. dollar drops relative to the yen).

The United States increases imports from Switzerland. Other things the same, the spot FX price of the Swiss franc is likely to (a) rise, or (b) drop. Choose (a) or (b).

Answer: (a) The increase in imports of Swiss products implies an increased demand for Swiss francs to make the purchases, so the FX price of the Swiss franc rises.

> Portfolio managers in the United States increase investment into Canadian securities. Other things the same, the spot FX price of the Canadian dollar is likely to (a) rise, or (b) drop. Choose (a) or (b).
>
> **Answer**: (a) The increase in investments into Canadian securities implies an increase in demand for Canadian dollars to make the purchases, so the FX price of the Canadian dollar rises.

In a flexible FX rate regime, a BOP deficit tends to be accompanied by a drop in the FX price of the country's currency, because the currency is being sold to import goods and/or make overseas investments. Often it has been the case that the United States has a deficit on trade (imports of goods higher than exports of goods), but a surplus on investment (more foreign investment into the United States than U.S. investment abroad). In this situation, the foreign investment into the United States is said to be *financing the trade deficit* and helping to prevent the U.S. dollar from depreciating. Information about BOP may be obtained from the U.S. Department of Commerce's Bureau of Economic Analysis: http://www.bea.gov/.

The *International Monetary Fund (IMF)* is an organization whose primary functions were originally to oversee the stability of the international FX system and to provide assistance to any member country in a short-term international monetary crisis. The IMF's role has been to lend funds to central banks. The IMF was also established to provide short-term monetary help to countries trying to develop modern economies for the first time or to rebuild economies after wars or revolutions, including World War II. The *World Bank*, also known as the *International Bank for Reconstruction and Development* provides capital to countries trying to develop or rebuild their economies. Unlike the IMF, the World Bank may issue bonds, in any currency, for purposes of raising capital.

The *Bank for International Settlements (BIS)* is an international organization that fosters cooperation among central banks and other agencies in pursuit of monetary and financial stability. The BIS headquarters is in Basel, Switzerland. Established in 1930, the BIS is the world's oldest international financial organization. Because its customers are central banks, the BIS does not accept deposits from, or provide financial services to, private individuals or corporate entities. The BIS makes international financial information available related to FX rates (http://www.bis.org/index.htm).

Intrinsic FX Rates and Speculation

For a given pair of currencies, the *intrinsic FX rate* is the "correct" FX rate based on economic fundamentals. In a truly *efficient FX market*, the actual FX rate and the intrinsic FX rate would be the same. In reality, many believe that an actual FX rate oscillates around the intrinsic FX rate. Actual FX rates are sometimes described as having two components: there is a permanent component that is the intrinsic FX rate; and there is a transitory component that is the deviation from the intrinsic FX rate. Just as with stocks, it is impossible in reality for anyone to know for sure the correct intrinsic FX rate.

Despite the diffculty in assessing an intrinsic FX rate, managers should be aware of when an actual FX rate is not likely to be equal to the intrinsic FX rate. Whether a currency is undervalued or overvalued may have a bearing on risk management and investment decisions. In subsequent chapters, we will examine some of the fundamental economic factors that should affect intrinsic FX rates. We'll also cover ways in which a manager can make an educated guess as to whether a currency is overvalued or undervalued.

Another important participant in the FX market is the speculator, who tries to make money on a view about the future direction of FX rates. Naturally, speculators account for supply and demand pressure on FX rates, beyond that fundamentally coming from the retail arena and central banks. Typically, speculators are private operators or trader–dealers employed by financial institutions. Some speculators are informed, whereas others are not. Informed speculators base their trading on good fundamental economic information. Informed speculators form a notion of how far an actual FX rate deviates from the intrinsic FX rate. If the perceived deviation of the actual FX rate from the intrinsic FX rate is large enough, informed speculators trade currencies to try to profit from this misalignment. Other speculators are uninformed; they ignore fundamental FX values and typically "chase trends" to try to profit. Informed speculators trading on solid fundamental information should drive an actual FX rate toward its intrinsic FX rate. Uninformed FX trading, like "trend chasing" not based on fundamentals, may drive actual FX rates away from intrinsic

FX rates. The speculation activity by corporate entities is said to have declined substantially. By contrast, the internet has made it easier for private speculators to trade in the FX market.

A central bank sometimes uses its FX reserves to buy the country's currency in the event that the central bank wants to "defend" its currency, that is, prevent the FX price of the currency from falling due to external selling. Speculators have sometimes tried to figure out when a central bank may be running low on its overall FX reserves, and hence, unable to support the value of its own currency in the FX market by using FX reserves to buy it. The speculators will then "attack" that currency by selling it in large quantity, hastening a crisis and devaluation, and profiting at the expense of the central bank. A history of central bank losses to speculators, culminating in a 1992 British pound crisis, may have been the reason that central banks curtailed direct intervention in the FX market somewhat after 1992. George Soros is a private speculator who has received much publicity, particularly in connection with the Asian crisis of the late 1990s.

Percentage Changes in FX Rates

To compute the percentage change in the spot FX price of a currency, you use FX rates expressed with that currency in the denominator. The percentage change in the spot FX price of the British pound over the period from time 0 to time N is denoted as $x_N^{\$/\pounds}$, and shown as equation (2.1). We will often use *lower case letters* to denote percentage-change variables.

Percentage Change in Spot FX Price of the Pound

$$x_N^{\$/\pounds} = (X_N^{\$/\pounds} - X_0^{\$/\pounds})/X_0^{\$/\pounds} \qquad (2.1)$$

For example, if the spot FX price of the pound at time 0 is $X_0^{\$/\pounds} =$ 1.60 $/£, and appreciates to 2.00 $/£ at time 1, the percentage change in the spot FX price of the pound is $x_1^{\$/\pounds} = (2.00 \ \$/\pounds - 1.60 \ \$/\pounds)/(1.60 \ \$/\pounds)$ = 0.25, or 25%. Often, we will ignore the time subscript when the percentage change is for a single period, and just use the notation $x^{\$/\pounds}$.

There is a slightly easier "short-cut" formula for computing the percentage change in the spot FX price of a currency, which we'll often use, as shown as equation (2.1a).

Percentage Change in Spot FX Price of the Pound
Shortcut

$$x_N^{\$/£} = X_N^{\$/£}/X_0^{\$/£} - 1 \qquad (2.1a)$$

In our example, we can use equation $(2.1a)$ to find the same percentage change in the FX price of the pound, $x^{\$/£} = (2.00\ \$/£)/(1.60\ \$/£) - 1 = 0.25$, or 25%.

Can you say the spot FX price of the U.S. dollar correspondingly depreciates by 25% relative to the pound? The answer is "approximately, but not exactly." Considering the percentage change in the FX price of the U.S. dollar relative to the pound requires you to use FX rates from the viewpoint of the U.S. dollar as the "denominator" currency. In this case, the spot FX rate changes from $X_0^{£/\$} = 1/X_0^{\$/£} = 1/(1.60\ \$/£) = 0.625\ £/\$$ to $X_1^{£/\$} = 1/(2.00\ \$/£) = 0.50\ £/\$$. The percentage change in the spot FX price of the U.S. dollar is $x^{£/\$} = (0.50\ £/\$)/(0.625\ £/\$) - 1 = -0.20$, a 20% depreciation of the U.S. dollar. Although the pound appreciates by 25% relative to the U.S. dollar, the U.S. dollar depreciates by only 20% relative to the pound.

Assume the spot FX rate for the Swiss franc goes from 1.50 Sf/$ to 1.25 Sf/$.

(a) Find the percentage change in the FX price of the U.S. dollar relative to the Swiss franc, and state whether this change is an appreciation or depreciation of the U.S. dollar.

(b) Find the percentage change in the FX price of the Swiss franc, and state whether the change is an appreciation or a depreciation of the Swiss franc.

Answers: (a) The percentage change in the FX price of the U.S. dollar is $x^{Sf/\$} = (1.25\ Sf/\$)/(1.50\ Sf/\$) - 1 = -0.1667$, or minus 16.67%. Thus, the FX price of the U.S. dollar depreciates by 16.67% relative to the Swiss franc. (b) The FX quotes must be reciprocated to find the percentage change in the FX price of the Swiss franc. Performing this reciprocation directly in the shorter percentage change formula, we have $x^{\$/Sf} = [1/(1.25\ Sf/\$)]/[1/(1.50\ Sf/\$)] - 1 = 0.20$, or a 20% appreciation in the FX price of the Swiss franc (relative to the U.S. dollar).

We can apply a formula that accurately relates the percentage FX changes from the two different currency perspectives. The formula with the U.S. dollar and the euro as the representative currencies is shown in equation (2.2):

Percentage Changes in Spot FX Rates: Different Perspectives

$$(1 + x^{\$/€})(1 + x^{€/\$}) = 1 \tag{2.2}$$

Equation (2.2) can also be restated as $(1 + x^{\$/€}) = 1/(1 + x^{€/\$})$, or equivalently $(1 + x^{€/\$}) = 1/(1 + x^{\$/€})$. Although equation (2.2) is valid for percentage changes over any horizon, it is common to regard $x^{\$/€}$ as an *annualized* percentage change.

Apply equation (2.2) to verify the answers to the previous problem, where the Swiss franc appreciated by 20% and the U.S. dollar depreciated by 16.67%.

Answer: $(1 + x^{\$/SFr})(1 + x^{SFr/\$}) = (1 + 0.20)(1 - 0.1667) = 1$.

Currency Conversions

To make sure you can use an FX rate in currency conversion calculations, say you want to convert an amount in U.S. dollars, $20,000, to yen, given an FX rate of 125 ¥/$. In this case, you should multiply the amounts, because the U.S. dollar symbol in the denominator of the FX rate will "cancel" with the U.S. dollar symbol of the currency amount, leaving the units for the answer in the numerator currency symbol of the FX rate, yen: $20,000(125 ¥/$) = ¥2,500,000 = ¥2.5 million.

Now suppose you are given a yen amount of, say, ¥500,000, to convert into U.S. dollars at the FX rate of 125 ¥/$. It would make no sense to multiply ¥500,000 by 125 ¥/$ because there is no cancellation of the yen symbol on the currency amount with the denominator currency symbol of the FX rate, the U.S. dollar. To perform the conversion of yen into U.S. dollars at an FX rate expressed in ¥/$, one can take either of two approaches.

One approach is to reciprocate the FX rate into direct terms from the United States point of view, that is, U.S. dollars per yen, which is 1/(125 ¥/$) = 0.008 $/¥, and then multiply ¥500,000 by the reciprocated FX rate. Thus, you would have ¥500,000 × (0.008 $/¥) = $4,000. Because the currency symbol of the amount, ¥, cancels with the denominator currency symbol (¥) in the FX rate, the answer is in U.S. dollars. The second approach is a shortcut. Simply divide ¥500,000 by the quoted FX rate, 125 ¥/$, as in ¥500,000/(125 ¥/$). Now the ¥ symbol in the amount cancels with the ¥ symbol in the numerator currency of the FX rate, while the denominator currency symbol, $, following the basic algebraic principle that a "denominator of a denominator" goes to the numerator and thus becomes the units for the answer: $4,000.

The FX rate for the euro is 1.60 $/€.

(a) You want to convert $1,000 to an equivalent amount in euros. What is amount in euros?

(b) You want to convert €1,000 to an equivalent amount in U.S. dollars. What is amount in U.S. dollars?

Answers: (a) $1,000/(1.60 $/€) = €625; (b) €1,000(1.60 $/€) = $1,600.

FX Transaction Exposure

In general, the volatility and uncertainty in FX rates creates a problem for companies that receive funds and make payments in foreign currencies. The uncertainty in the home currency value of a contracted foreign currency amount is called *FX transaction exposure*. Assume that a U.S. company has shipped products to Germany, and the terms call for payment of €3,000 6 months from now. Because the $/€ spot FX rate 6 months from now is unknown at the present, the amount of U.S. dollars that the euro receivable will ultimately provide is uncertain.

For example, if in 6 months' time the spot FX rate is 1.20 $/€, the euro inflow will be worth €3,000 × (1.20 $/€) = $3,600. If instead the spot FX rate 6 months from now turns out to be 1.30 $/€, the euro inflow will be worth €3,000 × (1.30 $/€) = $3,900. Figure 2.2 depicts the

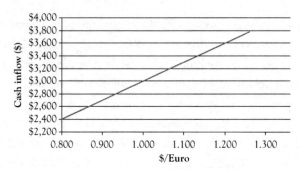

Figure 2.2. FX transaction exposure: Future receipt of €3,000.

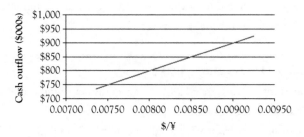

Figure 2.3. FX transaction exposure: Future payment of ¥100 million.

FX transaction exposure of a future euro receipt of €3,000, from the U.S. dollar point of view.

FX transaction exposure may be similarly associated with a future payable of an amount of foreign currency that is owed on services received or contracted. The higher the spot FX price of the foreign currency at the time the payment is made, the more home currency is necessary to make the payment, as shown in Figure 2.3. If a U.S. company owes ¥100 million due a year from now, and the spot FX rate turns out to be 125 ¥/$, the U.S. dollars owed will be $800,000. However, if the FX price of the yen is higher a year from now, at say an FX rate of 100 ¥/$, the amount of U.S. dollars owed will be higher, $1 million.

A U.S. exporter has a Swiss franc receivable. If the Swiss franc depreciates between now and the due date of the receivable, will the exporter be fortunate or unfortunate?

Answer: Unfortunate; the depreciation of the receivable currency implies fewer U.S. dollars for the exporter.

A U.S. importer has a Japanese yen payable. If the U.S. dollar depreciates (relative to the yen) between now and the due date of the payable, will the importer be fortunate or unfortunate?

Answer: Unfortunate; the depreciation of the U.S. dollar relative to the yen is an appreciation of the yen, and an appreciation of the payable currency implies that the importer will have to pay more U.S. dollars.

The FX rate for the Swiss franc declines from 1.50 Sf/$ to 1.20 Sf/$.
(a) You are due to receive Sf 15,000; do you have a windfall gain or loss?
(b) You are due to make a payment of Sf 15,000; do you have a windfall gain or loss?

Answers: The Swiss franc has appreciated, so you have (a) a windfall gain on the Swiss francs due to you, and (b) a windfall loss on the payment you are due to make. At 1.50 Sf/$, a Sf 15,000 payment is worth $10,000. At 1.20 Sf/$, a Sf 15,000 payment is worth $12,500.

FX transaction exposure underlies the problem known as the *importer–exporter dilemma*. Either the importer or the exporter faces risk, depending on the currency in which the price of traded goods is set. Consider a Eurozone supplier of parts to a U.S. manufacturer. If the supplier sets the parts prices in euros, the U.S. manufacturer faces the risk that the euro will appreciate, making the imported parts more expensive. Alternatively, if parts prices are set in U.S. dollars, the supplier faces the risk that the euro will appreciate (the U.S. dollar will depreciate) and will receive fewer euros for its parts.

ABC Co. is a U.S. manufacturer. ABC agrees to pay €5,000 upon delivery for materials from its Eurozone supplier, DEK Ltd. The spot FX rate is 1.20 $/€ when the order is placed and is 1.30 $/€ at the delivery time.
(a) What does ABC Co. expect to pay in U.S. dollars based on the spot FX rate when the materials are ordered? What does ABC actually pay?

(b) Assume the materials' price is instead set at $6,000, based on the spot FX rate when the deal is made, 1.20 $/€. How many euros does DEK expect based on the spot FX rate at the time of the order, and how many euros does DEK actually receive?

Answers: (a) ABC expects to pay $6,000, but actually pays €5,000 (1.30 $/€) = $6,500. (b) DEK expects to receive €5,000, but actually receives $6,000/(1.30 $/€) = €4,615.

Whether the pricing of an import–export deal is in the importer's currency or the exporter's currency, and thus which party has the FX risk, depends on the negotiation between the buyer and the seller. A distinct possibility in international trades is that the buyer and seller will negotiate to share the FX risk and the potential windfall FX gain, by making the pricing contingent on the spot FX rate that prevails at the time the goods are delivered. For example, the agreement could be to "split the difference," where the buyer pays the average of (a) the expected payment, and (b) the payment that would be made if the goods price is fixed in the seller's currency. In the ABC/DEK example, "split the difference" pricing means that ABC will pay ($6,000 + 6,500)/2 = $6,250, and thus DEK receives $6,250/(1.30 $/€) = €4,808. Thus, both companies have FX transaction exposure, but ABC has lower FX transaction exposure than if the goods price is in euros, and DEK has lower FX transaction exposure than if the goods price is in U.S. dollars. In the next example, the importer and exporter share the windfall gain of a depreciation of the euro.

Extend the previous example. When the spot FX rate is 1.20 $/€, the U.S. manufacturer ABC Co. agrees to "split the difference" goods pricing. If the spot FX rate is 1.00 $/€ at the delivery time, how much does ABC pay (in U.S. dollars), and how much does DEK receive (in euros)?

Answer: ABC would pay €5,000(1 $/€) = $5,000 if the goods price is fixed in euros. So ABC pays ($6,000 + 5,000)/2 = $5,500. DEK receives $5,500/(1 $/€) = €5,500. ABC pays less and DEK receives more than expected at the original spot FX rate of 1.20 $/€, because the FX risk is shared according to the agreement.

Gold and FX Rates

Gold has continued to be a means of settling international trade accounts between countries. If the United Kingdom has a BOP surplus with the United States, the Bank of England can then either hold the U.S. dollars as official FX reserves or redeem them at the U.S. Federal Reserve for gold (or for some of the Fed's official FX reserves of pounds). However, many central banks have been reducing their gold reserves in recent years, because gold does not earn interest while foreign currency can be held in the form of interest-bearing securities. Nowadays, gold represents only approximately 2% of the international reserves of the United States.

The *gold standard* for the exchange of currencies began before there were any national currencies, when trade was conducted by barter. The first widely accepted medium of exchange was gold, and merchants began to judge the value of all other commodities in terms of ounces of gold.

At some point, the volume of business transactions outgrew the supply of gold available to serve as a medium of exchange. To solve this problem, those holding large quantities of gold became bankers, printing, and circulating paper notes redeemable for gold. The gold notes became a convenient medium of exchange, and by lending gold to borrowers in the form of paper notes, more in gold notes were in circulation than was represented physically by the gold on hand in banks, "in reserve." Thus, quite a large volume of business transactions could be supported as if there were more gold on hand. The system worked, provided participants had confidence in banks to deliver gold against the notes on demand, and that not everyone tried to take physical delivery of gold at once.

Eventually, as paper money became nationalized, each country established a central bank to control its paper money supply. The system of paper notes expanded to checks and eventually to electronic balances, on the same principle as the gold reserve system: The physical supply of national paper money could be much lower than the amount circulated in the form of checks and electronic transfers. A bank, as part of a national financial system, is required to hold paper currency reserves and to provide paper money for deposit balances on demand, but the system is based on the notion that not everyone needs to hold the physical paper money at the same time.

Although it is now impractical, for some time banks were required to redeem paper money for gold on demand. Banks borrowed paper money from the central bank based on gold deposits. Under this gold standard system, the price at which a central bank would buy or sell gold to banks for paper money was a federal decision. In other words, a free market did not determine the price. The fact that countries' central banks maintained set prices for gold in their national currencies generally dictated FX rates. For example, the United States might set a rate of $20 per ounce of gold, and the British a rate of £4 per ounce. As long as the two nations maintained these set prices for the redemption of gold, the spot FX rate between the national paper currencies (and thus deposit balances) was fixed at 5 $/£.

Problems with the gold standard began in the chaotic twentieth century time of the world wars and the Great Depression. National governments often devalued national currencies relative to gold trying to gain a trade advantage over others. For example, the British government might decide to value an ounce of gold at £5 per ounce instead of £4 per ounce. If the United States maintained a gold price of $20 per ounce, the spot FX price of the pound devalued to 4 $/£. After the devaluation, those in the United Kingdom holding pound balances now would find U.S. goods more expensive and would thus tend to buy more at home. By the same token, those in the United States would find British goods less expensive and tend to import more from Britain. The British government might want this result for two reasons: (1) the trade surplus added gold to the British national treasury, and (2) more jobs would be created in their country by the increase in overseas demand for the relatively inexpensive British products.

However, the downside was that because people did not want to hold a currency if they thought it might be devalued, they tended to redeem for gold at that country's banks. Central banks of other countries would hold less of the currency as official FX reserves if there were some suspicion that a foreign central bank would close its gold window or devalue its currency by raising the official price for gold in terms of its own currency.

Eventually, the United States eliminated the national gold standard when it discontinued the redeemability of paper notes for gold. For a while, the United States continued to maintain a fixed U.S. dollar price for gold for the settlement of international trade accounts and for purchase of gold from U.S. citizens. This system, termed the *modified gold standard*, ended in the early 1970s when inflationary pressures forced the United States to quit backing the U.S. dollar with gold, and the price of gold was allowed to find its free market price. Since the end of the gold standard, the world has relied on *fiat money*, so-called because it is created by government fiat and backed only by the promises of central bankers to protect its value.

For convenience and protection, many countries' gold reserves are stored in the vault at the New York Federal Reserve. The use of gold for BOP settlements often simply involves the movement of gold bars from one country's gold cubicle to another's.

Summary Action Points

- Some basic supply and demand forces that cause volatility in FX rates are the international trade and investment activity by commercial parties, and the FX market participation by central banks, commercial banks, and speculators.
- A BOP deficit means that the country's total purchases of foreign goods plus its investments into foreign assets exceed the total purchases of the country's goods by foreigners plus investments by foreigners in the country's assets.
- An intrinsic FX rate is the correct FX rate based on economic fundamentals. Actual FX rates tend to oscillate around intrinsic FX rates.
- FX rate changes can create windfall gains or losses for those with receipts and payments in foreign currencies. This basic idea is called FX transaction exposure.

Glossary

Balance of payments deficit (surplus): A country in this condition has a net outflow (inflow) of currency, including gold.

Bank for International Settlements (BIS): An international organization that fosters cooperation among central banks and other agencies in pursuit of monetary and financial stability.

Efficient FX market: An ideal market in which actual FX rates are equal to the intrinsic FX values.

Fiat money: Currency created by government fiat and backed only by the promises of central bankers to protect its value.

Foreign currency reserves (or FX reserves): Holdings by a central bank in various currencies to facilitate international settlements and provide backing for its own currency.

Foreign direct investment (FDI): Investment into plant and subsidiaries in a foreign country, as distinct from international portfolio investment in securities.

FX broker: One who buys currency in the interbank market and, in turn, sells the currency at a markup to smaller players.

FX transaction exposure: The uncertainty in the home currency value of a contracted foreign currency amount.

Hard currency: A currency that holds its value because the country's economy is strong and growing, and not experiencing severe inflation and economic deterioration.

Importer–exporter dilemma: A risk problem for firms in international trade. Either the importer or the exporter faces risk, depending on the currency in which traded goods are priced, or both parties share the risk through a negotiated pricing agreement based on the FX rate at time of payment.

Interbank (FX) market: The wholesale international market for currency trading between major banks and financial institutions around the world.

International Bank for Reconstruction and Development (IBRD): See *World Bank.*

International Monetary Fund (IMF): An organization established by international agreement to help any member country in a short-term international monetary crisis.

Intrinsic FX rate: The "correct" FX rate based on economic fundamentals; the actual FX rate may not be equal to the intrinsic FX rate.

Modified gold standard: A system in the United States, now discontinued, of maintaining a fixed price for buying gold, but not redeeming notes for gold.

Portfolio investment: Investments in financial securities such as stocks, bonds as distinct from foreign direct investment.

Retail (FX) market: The market for currency exchange between banks and retail businesses and investment portfolios.

Soft currency: A currency that loses value because the country's economy is weak and experiencing inflation.

World Bank: An international agency that provides capital assistance to countries that are trying to develop or rebuild their economies. Also known as the *International Bank for Reconstruction and Development (IBRD)*.

Discussion Questions

1. Explain some reasons a currency of a flexible FX rate regime changes in FX price relative to another currency.
2. Discuss the roles of the following in the FX market: (a) the need to exchange currencies to conduct international business and for cross-border portfolio investments; (b) policies of national central banks; and (c) speculation.
3. What is the importer–exporter dilemma?

Problems

1. Assume that companies in the United States increase exports to Switzerland. Other things the same, the spot FX price of the Swiss franc is likely to (a) rise, or (b) drop. Choose (a) or (b).
2. Assume that investors in the United States decrease their investments in Japanese assets. Other things the same, the spot FX price of the yen is likely to (a) rise, or (b) drop. Choose (a) or (b).
3. Assume the spot FX rate for the British pound goes from 1.60 $/£ to 1.25 $/£.
   (a) Find the percentage change in the FX price of the U.S. dollar relative to the pound, and state whether this change is an appreciation or depreciation of the U.S. dollar.
   (b) Find the percentage change in the FX price of the pound, and state whether the change is an appreciation or a depreciation of the British pound.
4. The time-0 spot FX rate between the Swiss franc and the U.S. dollar is 1.50 Sf/$. The time-1 spot FX rate is 1.75 Sf/$.
   (a) What is the percentage change in the spot FX price of the Swiss franc (relative to the U.S. dollar)?
   (b) What is the percentage change in the spot FX price of the U.S. dollar (relative to the Swiss franc)?

5. Today's spot FX rate is 1.35 \$/€. A year from now, the spot FX rate turns out to be 1.20 \$/€.

   (a) Over the year, does the euro appreciate or depreciate (relative to the U.S. dollar)?

   (b) Over the year, does the U.S. dollar appreciate or depreciate (relative to the euro)?

   (c) What is the percentage change in the FX price of the U.S. dollar (relative to the euro)?

   (d) What is the percentage change in the FX price of the euro (relative to the U.S. dollar)?

6. The spot FX rate for the Swiss franc is 1.60 Sf/\$.

   (a) You want to convert \$1,000 to an equivalent amount in Swiss francs. What is amount in Swiss francs?

   (b) You want to convert Sf 1,000 to an equivalent amount in U.S. dollars. What is the amount in U.S. dollars?

7. A U.S. exporter has a 3-month Swiss franc receivable. If the spot FX rate changes from 1.25 Sf/\$ today to 1.35 Sf/\$ three months from now, will the exporter be fortunate or unfortunate?

8. A Japanese importer has a U.S. dollar payable. If the spot FX rate changes from 120 ¥/\$ to 100 ¥/\$ between now and the due date of the payable, will the importer be fortunate or unfortunate?

9. A U.S. company exports parts to a Korean manufacturer. When the spot FX rate is 1,180 ₩/\$, the companies agree to a price of ₩590 million for the parts, payable when the parts are delivered. Assume that when the parts are delivered, the spot FX rate is 1,000 ₩/\$.

   (a) How much does the U.S. firm expect to receive in U.S. dollars based on the spot FX rate when the parts were ordered? How much does the U.S. firm actually receive?

   (b) If the price had instead been set in U.S. dollars at \$500,000, how many won would the buyer have expected to pay based on the spot FX rate at the time of the order, and how many won are actually paid?

10. Extend problem 9. When the spot FX rate is 1,180 ₩/\$, the companies agree to a "split-the-difference" goods price policy. Assume that when the parts are delivered, the spot FX rate is 1,000 ₩/\$.

(a) How many won does the buyer expect to pay based on the FX rate at the time of the order, and how many won does the buyer actually pay?

(b) How much does the seller expect to receive in U.S. dollars based on the spot FX rate at the time of the order, and how much does the seller actually receive?

Answers to Problems

1. (b)

2. (b)

3. (a) The percentage change in the U.S. dollar is $x^{£/\$} = (0.80 £/\$)/(0.625 Sf/\$) - 1 = 0.28$, or 28%. Thus, the U.S. dollar appreciates by 28% relative to the British pound. (b) $x^{\$/£} = (1.25 \$/£)/(1.60 \$/£) - 1 = -0.22$, a 22% depreciation of the pound (vs. the U.S. dollar).

4. (a) $x^{\$/Sf} = -0.1428$, or −14.28%; (b) $x^{Sf/\$} = 0.1667$, or 16.67%.

5. (a) The euro depreciates; (b) the U.S. dollar appreciates; (c) the U.S. dollar appreciates by 12.5%; (d) the euro depreciates by 11.1%.

6. (a) $\$1,000 \times (1.60 Sf/\$) = Sf 1,600$; (b) $Sf 1,000/(1.60 Sf/\$) = \$625$.

7. Unfortunate

8. Fortunate

9. (a) $500,000; $590,000; (b) ₩590 million; ₩500 million

10. (a) ₩590 million; (590 million + 500 million)/2 = ₩545 million; (b) $500,000; ₩545 million/(1,000 ₩/$) = $545,000

CHAPTER 3

Purchasing Power Parity

A currency is misvalued when the actual foreign exchange (FX) rate is not equal to the intrinsic FX rate. In the global business environment, the success of a manager's strategic decisions may well depend on whether a currency is overvalued, undervalued, or correctly valued. So managers need to understand the basics of intrinsic FX rates.

In this chapter, we cover the connection between FX rates and goods prices, and the role of goods prices in intrinsic FX rates. You will learn about *long-run* intrinsic FX rates based on purchasing power.

FX Rate Changes and Foreign Demand for Goods

In principle and other things the same in a flexible FX rate system, a drop in the foreign demand for a country's goods tends to lead to a drop in the FX price of the country's currency, and vice versa. Now let's think about the other direction. How do FX rate changes affect foreign demand for a country's goods?

Other things the same, as the FX price of a country's currency rises, the country's goods become more expensive to foreign buyers. For example, if the euro appreciates from 1.25 $/€ to 1.40 $/€, a given Eurozone good is more expensive to a purchaser using U.S. dollars.

So, in principle, an increase in the FX price of the currency should tend to reduce the foreign demand for the goods. For example, if the spot FX rate changes from 120 ¥/$ to 100 ¥/$, a depreciation of the U.S. dollar and an appreciation of the yen, and other things stay the same, the United States' demand for Japanese goods should drop. The rise in the FX price of the yen (relative to the U.S. dollar) makes Japanese goods more expensive to U.S. buyers. As well, U.S. goods become less expensive to Japanese buyers, and thus U.S. exports to Japan are likely to increase.

If the spot FX rate changes from 1.25 Sf/$ today to 1.35 Sf/$, and other things stay the same, U.S. imports of goods from Switzerland are likely to (a) increase or (b) decrease. Choose (a) or (b).

Answer: (a) The FX price of the Swiss franc has fallen, making Swiss goods less expensive to U.S. buyers.

Because a *higher* FX price of a currency is a cause of lower foreign demand for the country's goods, which in turn leads to a *lower* FX price of the currency, we see the *self-stabilizing principle of FX rates*. As an example, assume the FX price of the British pound rises. Other things equal, U.S. importers are likely to buy fewer goods from United Kingdom, and U.K. importers are likely to buy more goods from U.S. sources. This shift in goods demand should tend to drive the FX price of the pound back down, in the opposite direction of the initial upward movement. Similarly, if the FX price of the pound initially drops, other things equal, U.S. importers are likely to buy more goods from United Kingdom, and U.K. importers are likely to buy fewer goods from U.S. sources. This shift in demand should drive the FX price of the pound back up, in the opposite direction of the initial FX rate change.

International Law of One Price

The price of a tradable good in one country should *theoretically* be equal to the price of the same good in another country, after adjusting for the FX rate. The principle called the *international law of one price* (*ILOP*) condition. To see this principle, let's use wheat as the representative tradable good. Denoting the price of a bushel of wheat in the United States at time N as $P_N^\$$ and the price of a bushel of wheat in the United Kingdom at time N as $P_N^\pounds$, the ILOP condition implies that the spot FX rate at time N *should be* $P_N^\$/P_N^\pounds$, as shown in equation (3.1). The I subscript in $X_{IN}^{\$/\pounds}$ denotes that the reference is to the *ILOP* spot FX rate, as opposed to the *actual* spot FX rate, which is denoted by only the time subscript, $X_N^{\$/\pounds}$.

International Law of One Price

$$X_{IN}^{\$/\pounds} = P_N^\$/P_N^\pounds \qquad (3.1)$$

For example, assume that at time N a bushel of wheat costs $P_N^\$ =$ $1.60 in the United States and $P_N^\pounds = \pounds 1.00$ in the United Kingdom. The ILOP condition says that the spot FX rate at time N should be $X_{IN}^{\$/\pounds} = \$1.60/\pounds1.00 = 1.60\ \$/\pounds$. At this FX rate, someone in the United States could buy a bushel for $1.60, or exchange the $1.60 into £1.00 and purchase a bushel in the United Kingdom for £1.00. Either way, the cost of wheat is the same.

Assume that a bushel of wheat costs $3.00 in the United States and €2.50 in France (in the Eurozone). What does the ILOP condition say should be the spot FX rate? Express your answer in the form of the accepted FX quotation convention.

Answer: Because the euro FX rate is conventionally expressed in American terms, we want the answer to be in $/€. Thus, $P^\$/P^\euro = \$3.00/€2.50 = 1.20\ \$/€$ is the spot FX rate that will make the cost of a bushel of wheat the same in both economies.

Assume that a bushel of wheat costs $3.00 in the United States and ¥300 in Japan, what does the ILOP condition say that the spot FX rate should be? Express your answer in the form of the accepted FX quotation convention.

Answer: Since the yen FX rate is conventionally expressed in European terms, we want the answer to be in ¥/$. Thus, $P^\yen/P^\$ = \yen300/\$3.00 = 100\ \yen/\$$ is the spot FX rate that will make the cost of a bushel of wheat the same in both economies.

FX Misvaluation and Goods Prices

Actual spot FX rates are often not equal to the ILOP ideal. The ILOP condition assumes no frictions to international trade, such as transportation costs and trade barriers (e.g., tariffs, quotas, and language/cultural barriers). In reality, these frictions can sometimes be significant. Moreover, actual spot FX rates and the prices of tradable goods may be misaligned with spot FX rates consistent with the ILOP condition, even beyond the level that is explainable by frictions in international trade. Stickiness in goods prices, in a world where actual FX rates fluctuate continually for many reasons, is an often-cited explanation for why the ILOP condition often does not describe actual spot FX rates.

To see an example of this last point, suppose we assume the ILOP condition holds at time 0 for wheat prices of $P_0^\$ = \$1.60$ and $P_0^£ = £1.00$. Thus the actual spot FX rate, $X_0^{\$/£}$, is assumed at time 0 to be equal to the ILOP FX rate, $X_{I0}^{\$/£} = 1.60$ \$/£. Then let us say that the actual spot FX rate subsequently rises to $X_I^{\$/£} = 2$ \$/£. (The reason for the rise is not important. Say it was because foreign investors moved funds into British investments, or there was some speculation by currency traders.) Before any adjustment in wheat prices takes place, a wheat buyer in the United Kingdom will now have the incentive to import wheat from the United States. Given the new actual spot FX rate of 2 \$/£, it will take £1.00, the equivalent of \$2.00, to buy a bushel of wheat in the United Kingdom but only £0.80, the equivalent of \$1.60, to buy a bushel in the United States. Correspondingly, wheat buyers in the United States will tend to not import any wheat from the United Kingdom, since \$1.60 will still buy a bushel in the United States, but will convert to only £0.80, which would buy less than a bushel in the United Kingdom. In principle, goods market arbitrageurs could profit by buying wheat in the United States and selling it in the United Kingdom.

Until and unless the actual FX rate changes again or one or both wheat prices adjust to reestablish the ILOP condition, the actual spot FX rate is misvalued in terms of purchasing power. The British pound is said to be *overvalued*, in the sense that the pound can purchase more overseas (in the United States) than the equivalent amount of U.S. dollars can purchase overseas (in the United Kingdom). Correspondingly, the U.S. dollar is *undervalued.*

So, using tradable goods prices as the measure of intrinsic FX value, an overvalued currency is one where the actual FX price of the currency is higher than the ILOP intrinsic FX value of the currency:

$$X^{\$/£} > X_I^{\$/£} \leftrightarrow \text{Overvalued British pound}$$

In the example above, the actual time-1 spot FX price of the pound is 2 \$/£, whereas the ILOP time-1 spot intrinsic FX value of the pound is

1.60 \$/£. Thus the British pound is overvalued at time 1. Similarly, an undervalued currency is one where the actual FX price of the currency is lower than the ILOP intrinsic FX value of the currency:

$$X^{£/\$} < X_I^{£/\$} \leftrightarrow \text{Undervalued U.S. dollar}$$

In the example above, the actual time-1 spot FX price of the U.S. dollar is 0.50 £/\$, whereas the ILOP time-1 spot intrinsic FX value of the U.S. dollar is 0.625 £/\$; the U.S. dollar is undervalued at time 1.

Assume that a bushel of wheat costs \$3.00 in the United States and €2.50 in France (in the Eurozone). Assume the actual spot FX rate is 1.50 \$/€. Choose (a), (b), or (c): Using wheat price as the standard of intrinsic FX value, the euro is (a) undervalued, (b) overvalued, or (c) neither (a) nor (b).

Answer: (b) Overvalued. The ILOP spot FX rate is $P^\$/P^€$ = \$3.00/ €2.50 = 1.20 \$/€. The actual spot FX price of the euro is higher than the ILOP intrinsic spot FX value of the euro, so the euro is overvalued. Thus, the U.S. dollar is undervalued. Note that €2.50 will buy exactly one bushel of wheat in France, but more than one bushel in the United States, because €2.50(1.50 \$/€) = \$3.75. And \$3.00 will buy exactly one bushel of wheat in the United States, but less than one bushel in France, because \$3.00/(1.50 \$/€) = €2.00.

Assume that the price of a bushel of wheat is \$3.00 in the United States and is ¥300 in Japan. Assume the actual spot FX rate is 80 ¥/\$. Choose (a), (b), or (c): Using the ILOP condition and wheat price as the standard of intrinsic FX value, the yen is (a) undervalued, (b) overvalued, or (c) neither (a) nor (b).

Answer: (b) Overvalued. The ILOP spot FX rate is $P^¥/P^\$$ = ¥300/\$3.00 = 100 ¥/\$. The actual spot FX price of the yen is higher than the ILOP intrinsic spot FX value of the yen, so the yen is overvalued. Thus, the U.S. dollar is undervalued. Note that ¥300 will buy exactly one bushel of wheat in Japan, but more than one bushel in the United States, because ¥300/(80 ¥/$) = $3.75. And $3.00 will buy exactly one bushel of wheat in the United States, but less than one bushel in Japan, because $3.00(80 ¥/$) = ¥240.

The theoretical argument behind the ILOP condition is that if the condition does not hold, significant trading activity should create substantial pressure on both FX rates and goods prices to quickly realign according to the ILOP condition. The high relative demand for goods from the country of the undervalued currency, and for that country's currency to buy the goods, should result in both higher goods prices in that country and, more immediately, an appreciation of that country's currency. That is, the application of the self-stabilizing principle implies that FX misvaluations should self-correct. In the ILOP *theory*, the self-stabilizing principle of FX rates is very strong and immediate. But in *reality*, corrections of ILOP violations are slow, and so actual spot FX rates may often be misvalued relative to tradable goods prices for long periods of time. However, as long as a misvaluation between an FX rate and goods prices persists, other things the same, there should be a tendency for the overvalued currency to continue to gradually depreciate and the undervalued currency to continue to gradually appreciate.[1]

Be aware that the terms *strong* and *weak* are frequently applied inconsistently in FX markets. Sometimes a "strong" currency is intended to be synonymous with an "overvalued" currency (and "weak" means "undervalued"). Other times, "strong" is used to describe a currency that is appreciating or has appreciated. Confusion may occur if a currency that is undervalued is appreciating (correcting); the currency would be weak in the first sense, but simultaneously strong in the second sense.

Purchasing Power and Trade Balance

By definition, a country that imports more than it exports over a period of time has a *trade deficit* for that time period. The opposite of a trade deficit is a *trade surplus*, which is an excess of the monetary value of exported goods over imported goods over a period of time. The trade balance is one of the two major components of the Balance of Payments, with the other being the balance on capital account for portfolio investment and foreign direct investment.

One factor affecting trade balances is whether there is any FX misvaluation. Other things equal, an economy whose currency is overvalued in terms of goods prices should have a relatively high demand for foreign goods, and its own goods should be in relatively low demand by other countries. So, other things the same, a country with an overvalued currency should tend to have a trade deficit, that is, import more goods than it exports (measured in a currency, for example, billions of U.S. dollars). And a country with an undervalued currency should tend to have a trade surplus, that is, export a higher monetary value of goods than it imports.

In the situation of our earlier example, depicted in Figure 3.1, the actual spot FX rate is 2.00 \$/£ (= 0.50 £/\$) but the ILOP spot FX rate is 1.60 \$/£ (= 0.625 £/\$). So the British pound is overvalued and the U.S. dollar is undervalued in terms of the prices of tradable goods. The United Kingdom trade deficit that results is shown by higher imports than exports. The United States trade surplus is shown by larger exports than imports.

However, the real world does not always reflect simple principles. During 2003–2007, for example, the euro was overvalued versus the U.S. dollar using the purchasing power standard of FX value, yet the United States continued to have a trade deficit with the Eurozone, the opposite direction of trade imbalance that the ILOP theory would suggest. Moreover, the extent of the euro's overvaluation grew throughout this time period. Warren Buffett said in March 2008 that the euro would continue

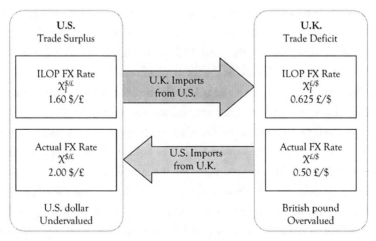

Figure 3.1. Goods prices and trade flow.

to appreciate as long as the United States continues to import more from the Eurozone than it exports.

Of course, FX misvaluation is not the only cause of a trade imbalance, but an understanding of the impact of FX misvaluation is useful. You can also reason that as the FX price of a currency drops, the country's trade balance should improve; a surplus should go higher and a deficit should go lower. The reverse should hold for an increase in the FX price of the currency. But in reality, there is also an effect called the *J-Curve*. Given a drop in the FX price of a currency, the J-Curve describes the tendency for a country's trade balance to first drop and then to begin to rise only after some time passes. The reason for the initial drop in trade balance is the inertia of orders for imports and exports along with the drop in the currency's FX price; the monetary value of the imports initially rises. As time passes, the levels of physical imports and exports shift, and eventually, the trade balance rises.

Note that a country with a strong economy, with high productivity and growth, may experience a trade deficit as a natural consequence. Due to the bright economic scenario, foreign capital is invested, driving up the spot FX price of the domestic currency. As this happens while goods prices are sticky, the domestic currency becomes overvalued in purchasing power terms. Then a trade deficit may result from use of the overvalued currency to import goods from abroad relatively cheaply. In this case, the trade deficit does not seem like such a bad thing; it is a natural consequence of an economy experiencing (and expecting) strong productivity and growth. The large U.S. trade deficit in the 1980s may have been an example of this sort of scenario. During the early 1980s, investment was coming to the United States from abroad. As the foreign investment demand for the U.S. dollar drove up its FX price, the U.S. dollar became overvalued in terms of goods prices. So the U.S. trade deficit may not be surprising.

But a trade deficit does not necessarily reflect a strong economy. In the 1990s, the Thai baht was overvalued. The baht had been supported and stabilized by the Thai central bank for the specific purpose of attracting foreign investment. Thailand incurred a trade deficit, and the hoped-for economic results of the investment never materialized. As foreign investors began to realize the situation and disinvested, and as the Thai central bank (and other Southeast Asian central banks helping defend the baht, like Malaysia and Indonesia) began to run out of FX reserves, the baht collapsed, starting a period remembered as "the Asian currency crisis."

Sometimes we see government policy to keep the FX price of a currency undervalued to try to generate trade surpluses, because exporting more than importing should help increase domestic jobs. This is the strategy that Japan followed and that China has been said to have followed recently. Although these cases are significant, concern over trade imbalances (deficits and surpluses) is less than in the days of *mercantilism*, where countries vie to "win," economically, over others in international trade. Instead, in the integrated global economy, countries' economies are interdependent, and trade becomes imbalanced at times as part of the natural development of the global economy.

Another reason that concern over trade imbalances has subsided somewhat is the global use of hard currencies. For example, U.S. dollars sent to countries outside the United States for imports are not always returned for gold or official FX reserves. Instead, U.S. dollars often serve more or less as an international currency. If U.S. officials were to try to create a depreciation of the U.S. dollar to correct a trade deficit, confidence in the U.S. dollar as international currency would drop.[2]

Absolute Purchasing Power Parity

The *Absolute Purchasing Power Parity (APPP) condition* is an economic theory of the long-run intrinsic FX rate. The theory is similar to the ILOP principle, but relates to general baskets of consumption goods, including both tradable and nontradable goods. That is, the difference between the ILOP and the APPP condition is that the ILOP condition refers to parity between FX rates and *tradable goods* prices, whereas the APPP condition refers to parity between FX rates and a *general index* of goods prices, including nontradable goods prices.

Equation (3.2) shows that the APPP condition is similar to the ILOP principle in equation (3.1), except that we use (a) a "P" subscript in the FX rate to denote that the rate is the purchasing power parity FX rate; and (b) a "B" subscript with the prices to denote that the prices in the APPP condition are for a *basket* of goods, or for a good that represents the price level of general consumption in the economy.

Absolute Purchasing Power Parity

$$X_{PN}{}^{\$/£} = P_{BN}{}^{\$}/P_{BN}{}^{£} \qquad (3.2)$$

The APPP approach to FX valuation works the same as the ILOP approach. An overvalued currency is one where the actual FX price of the currency is higher than the APPP FX value of the currency: $X^{\$/£} > X_P{}^{\$/£}$ implies an overvalued pound. Similarly, an undervalued currency is one where the actual FX price of the currency is lower than the APPP FX value of the currency: $X^{£/\$} < X_P{}^{£/\$}$ implies an undervalued U.S. dollar.

A popular yardstick of FX valuation in terms of purchasing power is the *Economist's* Big Mac Index, based on McDonalds "Big Mac" prices around the globe. The idea of the Big Mac Index is that a Big Mac is a representative good, and that we can compare Big Mac prices of various economies to gauge the degree of misvaluation in actual spot FX rates.

Exhibit 3.1 shows some data for *Economist* analysis for January 31, 2013, obtained from http://www.economist.com/content/big-mac-index. The first column shows local currency prices of a Big Mac. The third column converts the local prices into U.S. dollars using the actual spot FX rates shown in the second column. The fourth column shows APPP spot FX rates based on Big Mac prices in local currency. For instance, dividing the Japanese Big Mac price (¥320) by the American one ($4.37) gives an APPP spot FX rate of 73.23 ¥/$, using equation (3.2). The actual spot FX rate of 91.07 ¥/$, representing a higher FX price of the U.S. dollar, implies that the U.S. dollar is overvalued against the yen, and the yen is undervalued against the U.S. dollar (by almost 20%), basing intrinsic FX value on Big Mac prices.

The last column in Exhibit 3.1 gives the misvaluation of the actual spot FX price of the currency as a percent of the APPP FX value. For the Euro Area, the computation is (1.36 $/€)/(1.217 $/€) − 1 = 0.1175, representing an 11.75% overvaluation of the euro. For the yen, which is expressed in European terms, the calculation is [1/(91.07 ¥/$)]/[1/(73.23 ¥/$)] − 1 = −0.1959, a 19.59% undervaluation of the Japanese yen.

It is useful to see that the same percentage misvaluation of a currency may be found using the ratio of the converted Big Mac price in the third column to the Big Mac price in the United States, $4.37. For the euro, we

Exhibit 3.1. Big Mac Purchasing Power Parity Index (Raw)

Country	Big Mac local	Actual FX rate[a]	Big Mac price ($)	APPP FX rate[a]	Raw % FX misvalue
United States	4.37		4.37		
Argentina	19.00	4.98	3.82	4.35	−12.58
Australia	4.70	0.96	4.90	1.08	12.21
Brazil	11.25	1.99	5.64	2.58	29.22
Britain	2.69	1.58	4.25	1.62	−2.73
Canada	5.41	1.00	5.39	1.24	23.51
Chile	2050.00	471.75	4.35	469.39	−0.50
China	16.00	6.22	2.57	3.66	−41.2
Colombia	8600.00	1773.18	4.85	1969.14	11.05
Costa Rica	2200.00	500.83	4.39	503.73	0.58
Czech Republic	70.33	18.89	3.72	16.10	−14.77
Denmark	28.50	5.50	5.18	6.53	18.69
Egypt	16.00	6.69	2.39	3.66	−45.20
Euro area	3.59	1.36	4.88	1.217	11.75
Hong Kong	17.00	7.76	2.19	3.89	−49.83
Hungary	830.00	217.47	3.82	190.04	−12.61
India	89.00	53.40	1.67	20.38	−61.83
Indonesia	27939.00	9767.50	2.86	6397.18	−34.51
Israel	14.90	3.72	4.00	3.41	−8.40
Japan	320.00	91.07	3.51	73.27	−19.59
Latvia	1.69	0.52	3.28	0.39	−24.90
Lithuania	7.80	2.54	3.07	1.79	−29.81
Malaysia	7.95	3.08	2.58	1.82	−40.96
Mexico	37.00	12.74	2.90	8.47	−33.49
New Zealand	5.20	1.20	4.32	1.19	−0.98
Norway	43.00	5.48	7.84	9.85	79.56
Pakistan	290.00	97.67	2.97	66.40	−32.01
Peru	10.00	2.56	3.91	2.29	−10.54
Philippines	118.00	40.60	2.91	27.02	−33.45
Poland	9.10	3.09	2.94	2.08	−32.61
Russia	72.88	30.05	2.43	16.69	−44.46

(Continued)

Exhibit 3.1. Big Mac Purchasing Power Parity Index (Raw) (Continued)

Country	Big Mac local	Actual FX rate[a]	Big Mac price ($)	APPP FX rate[a]	Raw % FX misvalue
Saudi Arabia	11.00	3.75	2.93	2.52	−32.84
Singapore	4.50	1.23	3.64	1.03	−16.56
South Africa	18.33	9.05	2.03	4.20	−53.61
South Korea	3700.00	1085.48	3.41	847.19	−21.95
Sri Lanka	350.00	126.45	2.77	80.14	−36.62
Sweden	48.40	6.35	7.62	11.08	74.54
Switzerland	6.50	0.91	7.12	1.49	63.14
Taiwan	75.00	29.50	2.54	17.17	−41.79
Thailand	87.00	29.76	2.92	19.92	−33.05
Turkey	8.45	1.77	4.78	1.93	9.39
UAE	12.00	3.67	3.27	2.75	−25.19
Ukraine	19.00	8.14	2.33	4.35	−46.58
Uruguay	105.00	19.28	5.45	24.04	24.70
Venezuela	39.00	4.29	9.08	8.93	107.93

[a]In American terms; All other FX rates in European terms.

get \$4.88/\$4.37 − 1 = 0.1167, or 11.67%. For the yen, we get \$3.51/\$4.37 − 1 = −0.1968, or −19.68%. The slight differences between these answers and the ones above are due to rounding. (Algebraically, you get this approach by multiplying the Big Mac price in euros times both the numerator and denominator in the expression, $X^{\$/\euro}/X_P^{\$/\euro}$.)

So the percentage misvaluation of a currency is found by using either (a) the ratio of the actual American terms FX rate to the APPP FX rate, or equivalently, (b) the ratio of the economy's Big Mac price in U.S. dollars to the Big Mac price in the United States. Letting $P_{\pounds BN}^{\$}$ denote the foreign Big Mac price converted into U.S. dollars at the actual spot FX rate, that is, $P_{\pounds BN}^{\$} = P_{BN}^{\pounds}(X_N^{\$/\pounds})$, we get equation (3.3).

Percentage Misvaluation of British Pound

$$X_N^{\$/\pounds} / X_{PN}^{\$/\pounds} - 1 = P_{\pounds BN}^{\$} / P_{BN}^{\$} - 1 \qquad (3.3)$$

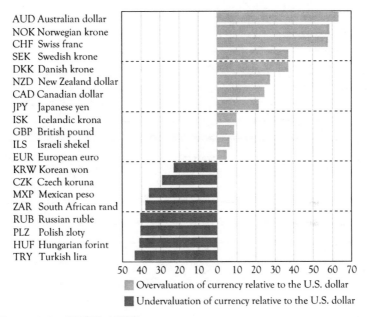

Figure 3.2. OECD APPP.

Source: OECD Pacific FX Service PPP reference year: 2011

The last column in Exhibit 3.1 says that the Chinese yuan is undervalued by 41.2%, using Big Mac prices as the basis for APPP.

(a) Verify the 41.2% undervaluation of the Chinese yuan using the actual FX rate and the APPP FX rate.

(b) Verify the 41.2% undervaluation of the Chinese yuan using the Chinese Big Mac price (in U.S. dollars) and the U.S. Big Mac price.

Answers: (a) $[1/(6.22 \text{ ¥/\$})]/[1/(3.66 \text{ ¥/\$})] - 1 = -0.412$, a 41.2% undervaluation of the Chinese yuan; (b) $\$2.57/\$4.37 - 1 = -0.412$, a 41.2% undervaluation of the Chinese yuan.

Studies have shown that there is a gradual adjustment process of FX APPP misvaluations, but that the process can be *very* gradual. The consensus of empirical researchers is that the half-life of convergence to parity is three to five years. Several academic studies have found that the Big Mac index is surprisingly useful in tracking gradual FX changes over the longer term. One researcher finds that after correcting for currency-specific

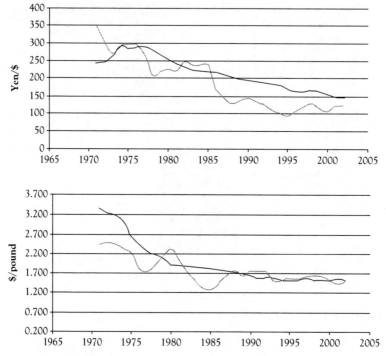

Figure 3.3. APPP spot FX rates versus actual spot FX rates. The dark curves are the APPP FX rates, using GDP; the light curves are average actual FX rates.

Source: OECD.

constants, "a 10% undervaluation according to the Big Mac standard in one year is associated with a 3.5% appreciation the following year."[3]

For those who think that the Big Mac approach to APPP is too "lighthearted," the *Organization for Economic Cooperation and Development (OECD)* also publishes information on APPP FX rates, but the OECD uses a broad basket of consumption goods. The OECD is an international organization that fosters economic development. The OECD has 30 member countries and active relationships with 70 others. The organization is best known for publications and statistics, including individual country surveys and reviews. The PPP information is at the Web site: http://www.oecd.org/std/prices-ppp/purchasingpowerparitiesppps data.htm. Figure 3.2 shows some FX valuation results for January 2013 for some currencies (relative to the U.S. dollar) using OECD's approach. This chart was found on the Web page: http://fx.sauder.ubc.ca/PPP.html.

Figure 3.3 uses historical OECD data to compare graphically actual spot FX rates for the pound and the yen and the corresponding APPP FX rates. One can see how the actual FX rate fluctuates around the APPP FX rate. We can think of the actual FX rates as fluctuating around the long-run intrinsic FX value.

Interestingly, a study has shown that the Big Mac approach to APPP is highly correlated with the seemingly more "official" consumer price index approach.[4]

Summary Action Points

- FX misalignments in terms of tradable goods prices could have implications for trade balances. Other things equal, a currency that is overvalued in terms of the ILOP may lead to a trade deficit and an undervalued currency may lead to a trade surplus.
- The APPP condition is a well-known standard of long-run intrinsic FX rates in terms of good prices.
- Using either the *Economist's* Big Mac Index or OECD data, actual spot FX rates are often observed to deviate from the long-run intrinsic FX rates implied by the APPP condition.
- Models of intrinsic FX rates are useful even if they don't "fit" the data, because we get an idea of whether a currency is misvalued and thus may be due for a correction.

Glossary

Absolute purchasing power parity (APPP): A theory that the price of a broad basket of consumption goods in one country should be equal to the price of a similar basket in another country, after adjusting for the FX rate.

International law of one price (ILOP): The principle that the price of a tradable good in one country should theoretically be equal to the price of the same good in another country, after adjusting for the FX rate.

J-Curve: Given a drop in the FX price of a currency, a country's trade balance tends to first drop and later rise.

Organization for Economic Cooperation and Development (OECD):
An international organization that fosters economic development.

Overvalued currency: A currency with an actual FX price is higher than its intrinsic FX value.

Strong currency: An expression with two interpretations: a currency that is overvalued or a currency that has been appreciating.

Trade deficit: The amount by which the value of a country's imported goods exceeds the value of its exported goods.

Trade surplus: The amount by which the value of a country's exported goods exceeds the value of its imported goods.

Undervalued currency: A currency with an actual FX price is lower than its intrinsic FX value.

Weak currency: An expression with two interpretations: A currency that is undervalued or a currency that has been depreciating.

Discussion Questions

1. Explain the self-stabilizing principle for FX rates.
2. Discuss the difference between the ILOP and APPP conditions.
3. Is a weak U.S. dollar good, bad, or neutral for the U.S. economy? Discuss this question and its CNBC poll results (11/19/03): 37% good; 47% bad; and 16% neutral.
4. Explain how a currency that is weak in the sense that it has been depreciating could also be strong in the sense that it is overvalued.

Problems

1. If the spot FX rate changes from 1.55 $/£ today to 1.65 $/£, and other things stay the same, United States imports from the United Kingdom are likely to (a) increase or (b) decrease. Choose (a) or (b).
2. If the spot FX rate changes from 100 ¥/$ to 120 ¥/$, and other things stay the same, U.S. exports to Japan are likely to (a) increase or (b) decrease. Choose (a) or (b).
3. If the spot FX rate changes from 100 ¥/$ to 120 ¥/$, and other things stay the same, U.S. imports from Japan are likely to (a) increase or (b) decrease. Choose (a) or (b).

4. If a bushel of wheat costs $3.00 in the United States and ¥240 in Japan, what does the ILOP condition says that the spot FX rate should be?

5. Assume that a bushel of wheat costs $3.00 in the United States and ¥240 in Japan. Assume the actual spot FX rate is 100 ¥/$. Choose (a), (b), or (c): Using wheat price as the standard of intrinsic FX value, the yen is (a) undervalued, (b) overvalued, or (c) neither (a) nor (b).

6. Assume that a bushel of wheat costs $3.00 in the United States and ¥300 in Japan. Assume the actual spot FX rate is 75 ¥/$. Circle (a), (b), or (c): Using wheat price as the standard of intrinsic FX value, the yen is: (a) undervalued; (b) overvalued; or (c) neither (a) nor (b).

7. Other things the same, if the U.S. dollar is overvalued relative to the Swiss franc in terms of tradable goods prices, the United States is likely to (a) import more goods from Switzerland than it exports to Switzerland, (b) export more goods to Switzerland than it imports from Switzerland, or (c) both. Choose (a), (b), or (c).

8. Other things the same, if the U.S. dollar is undervalued relative to the Swiss franc in terms of tradable goods prices, Switzerland is likely to (a) import more goods from United States than it exports to the United States, (b) export more goods to the United States than it imports from United States, or (c) both. Choose (a), (b), or (c).

For problems 9–11: Assume that the price of a bushel of wheat is €2 in Europe and is $3.00 in the United States. Assume the actual current spot FX rate is 1.40 $/€.

9. Using wheat prices as the benchmark for intrinsic FX value, choose (a), (b), or (c): (a) the U.S. dollar is undervalued against the euro; (b) the U.S. dollar overvalued against the euro; (c) cannot tell if the currencies are misvalued.

10. Choose (a), (b), or (c): Other things equal, (a) the United States is likely to have a trade deficit versus the Eurozone; (b) the United States is likely to have a trade surplus versus the Eurozone; (c) there should be no trade imbalance between the United States and the Eurozone.

11. Other things equal, over the coming year, (a) the spot FX price of the euro is likely to appreciate relative to the U.S. dollar; (b) the spot FX

price of the euro is likely to depreciate relative to the U.S. dollar; (c) there will be no tendency for the spot FX rate to change in either direction.

12. The last column in Exhibit 3.1 says that the Brazilian real was over-valued by 29.22% on January 31, 2013, using Big Mac prices as the basis for APPP. (a) Verify the 29.22% overvaluation of the Brazilian real using the actual FX rate and the APPP FX rate. (b) Verify the 29.22% overvaluation of the Brazilian real using the U.S. and Brazilian Big Mac prices (in U.S. dollars).

Answers to Problems

1. (b) The British pound rises, so U.K. products cost more to U.S. buyers.
2. (b) The FX price of the yen drops, making Japanese products cost less to U.S. buyers and making U.S. products cost more to Japanese buyers.
3. (a) Increase.
4. ¥240/$3 = 80 ¥/$.
5. (a) Undervalued. The ILOP spot FX rate is $P^{¥}/P^{\$} = ¥240/\$3.00 = 80$ ¥/$. The actual spot FX price of the yen is lower than the ILOP spot FX value of the yen, so the yen is undervalued. Thus, the U.S. dollar is overvalued. Note that ¥240 will buy exactly one bushel of wheat in Japan, but less than one bushel in the United States, since ¥240/(100 ¥/$) = $2.40. And $3.00 will buy exactly one bushel of wheat in the United States, but more than one bushel in Japan, since $3.00(100 ¥/$) = ¥300.
6. (b) Overvalued.
7. (a)
8. (a)
9. (b) The APPP spot FX rate is 1.50 $/€, so that the euro is currently undervalued, and the U.S. dollar is overvalued.
10. (a) The overvalued U.S. dollar should lead to a trade deficit for the United States, all else equal.

11. (a) The euro is undervalued, and so should appreciate, other things equal.
12. (a) [1/(1.99 Br/$)]/[1/(2.58 Br/$)] − 1 = 0.296, a 29.6% overvaluation of the Brazilian real, which differs from 29.22% due to rounding;
    (b) $5.64/$4.37 − 1 = 0.291, a 29.1% overvaluation of the Brazilian real, which differs from 29.22% due to rounding.

CHAPTER 4

Extensions of Purchasing Power Parity

In this chapter, we cover some extensions to the connection between goods prices and foreign exchange (FX) rates and the role of goods prices in determining intrinsic FX rates. First, we cover how inflation rates affect intrinsic FX rates. We'll apply this idea to understand how FX misvaluations occur in a setting where FX rates are fixed. Second, we cover an adjusted version of absolute purchasing power parity (APPP), where the adjustment is based on an economy's per-capita gross domestic product (GDP).

Relative Purchasing Power Parity

There is an extension of the international law of one price (ILOP) and APPP conditions that has to do with FX rate movements over time. This dynamic version of the theory relates FX rate changes to relative inflation rates, where "inflation rate" refers to the percentage change in goods prices. The dynamic version is known as the *relative purchasing power parity (RPPP) condition*. To explain the RPPP idea, we'll use wheat as the representative good, so the percentage change in the price of wheat in a country represents the inflation rate in that country.

Denote the U.S. inflation rate as $p^\$$ and the U.K. inflation rate as $p^\pounds$, noting our convention to use lower case letters for percentage changes. If the bushel prices of wheat at time 0 are $P_0^\$$ and $P_0^\pounds$, then the bushel prices of wheat at time 1 will be $P_1^\$ = P_0^\$(1 + p^\$)$ and $P_1^\pounds = P_0^\pounds(1 + p^\pounds)$, respectively. It may help to think of the inflation rates as pertaining to a unit of time, say, one year. For example, assume wheat prices at time 0 of $P_0^\$ = 2.00 per bushel in the U.S. and $P_0^\pounds = \pounds 1.00$ per bushel in the United Kingdom, and that the U.S. inflation rate is 6% (per year) and the U.K. inflation rate is 3% (per year). Then the new price of wheat in a year will be $2.00(1.06) = \$2.12$ in the United States and $£1.00(1.03) = £1.03$ in the United Kingdom.

The APPP condition says that the spot FX rate at time 0 should be $X_{P0}^{\$/£} = \$2.00/£1.00 = 2.00\ \$/£$, and that the new spot FX rate at time 1 should be $X_{P1}^{\$/£} = \$2.12/£1.03 = 2.06\ \$/£$. Despite the appreciation of the FX price of the pound (and the depreciation of the U.S. dollar), the U.S. dollar/pound spot FX rate is correctly valued in terms of wheat prices at both the beginning and ending times. That is, if the APPP condition holds at both times, there is no FX misvaluation in purchasing power terms, despite the change in the nominal FX price of the currencies. The RPPP condition, in terms of intrinsically correct spot FX rates at time 0 and time 1, can be expressed as equation (4.1).[1]

Relative Purchasing Power Parity
FX Rate Form

$$X_{P1}^{\$/£} = X_{P0}^{\$/£}[(1 + p^{\$})/(1 + p^{£})] \qquad (4.1)$$

Equation (4.1) follows a convention to put the time-1 FX rate on the left-hand side. With the time-0 FX rate on the right-hand side, the inflation rates in the bracket term obey the following format:

The inflation rate in the numerator of the bracket is the inflation rate of the currency of the numerator of the FX rate.

To grasp the logic behind equation (4.1), think in terms of the logic flow in Figure 4.1, with time 0 on the left and time 1 on the right, and

	Date		
	0		1
Currency			
U.S. dollars	$P_0^{\$}$	$x\,(1 + p^{\$})$ =	$P_1^{\$} = P_0^{\$}(1 + p^{\$})$
	$X_{P0}^{\$/£}$		$X_{P1}^{\$/£} = P_1^{\$}/P_1^{£} = X_{P0}^{\$/£}(1 + p^{\$})/(1 + p^{£})$
U.K. pounds	$P_0^{£} = P_0^{\$}/X_{P0}^{\$/£}$	$x\,(1 + p^{£})$ =	$P_1^{£} = P_0^{\$}(1 + p^{£})/X_{P0}^{\$/£}$

Figure 4.1. Logic flow of the relative purchasing power parity condition in equation (4.1).

with U.S. dollars on the top and British pounds on the bottom. Start at the top left with an amount of U.S. dollars at time 0 that will buy a bushel in the United States, $P_0^\$$. If the APPP FX rate holds at time 0, you can convert $P_0^\$$ into the amount of British pounds at time 0 (downward on the left) that will buy a bushel in the United Kingdom, $P_0^\pounds = P_0^\$/X_{P0}^{\$/\pounds}$. Moving to the right from the top left and thus going forward in time, the price of a bushel in the United States at time 1 is $P_0^\$(1 + p^\$)$. Moving to the right from the bottom left, it will take $P_1^\pounds = P_0^\$(1 + p_\pounds)/X_{P0}^{\$/\pounds}$ to buy a bushel in the United Kingdom at time 1. Thus if the APPP FX rate holds at time 1, then $X_{P1}^{\$/\pounds} = P_1^\$/P_1^\pounds$, which we see in bold on the right is equal to $X_{P0}^{\$/\pounds}(1 + p^\$)/(1 + p^\pounds)$, the FX rate form of the RPPP condition in equation (4.1).

We can also express the RPPP condition in percentage form. Let $x_P^{\$/\pounds}$ denote the percentage change in the APPP spot FX rate. That is, $x_P^{\$/\pounds} = X_{P1}^{\$/\pounds}/X_{P0}^{\$/\pounds} - 1$. Thus an alternative expression of the RPPP condition is in equation (4.2). As seen in the percentage version of RPPP in equation (4.2), the percentage change in a spot FX rate that is correctly valued in terms of good prices is based on the inflation rate differential, $(1 + p^\$)/(1 + p^\pounds)$.

Relative Purchasing Power Parity
Percentage Form

$$1 + x_P^{\$/\pounds} = (1 + p^\$)/(1 + p^\pounds) \qquad (4.2)$$

To apply equations (4.1) and (4.2) in an example, assume that the spot $/€ FX rate at time 0 is 1.15 $/€, and that the APPP condition holds. Assume that over the next year, the inflation rate in the Eurozone is 5% and in the United States 3%. The time-1 APPP spot FX rate, according to the RPPP condition of equation (4.1), should be (1.15 $/€)(1.03/1.05) = 1.128 $/€. Using equation (4.2), the percentage change in the APPP spot FX rate, if the RPPP condition holds, should be $x_P^{\$/€} = 1.03/1.05 - 1 = -0.019$, or −1.9%. That is, the spot FX price of the euro should drop by 1.9%. As a consistency check, we verify the new FX rate found using equation (4.1) with the percentage FX change found using equation (4.2): (1.15 $/€)(1 + $x_P^{\$/€}$) = (1.15 $/€)(1 − 0.019) = 1.128 $/€. In this scenario, the euro depreciates by 1.9% in intrinsic FX value from 1.15 $/€ to 1.128 $/€, offsetting the higher inflation in Europe. The only way for the APPP condition to hold, after the goods price increase in Europe, is for the U.S. dollar to buy more euros; so the U.S. dollar appreciates and the euro depreciates.

Of course, the two versions of the RPPP condition may also be expressed in European terms: $X_{P1}^{£/\$} = X_{P0}^{£/\$}[(1 + p^£)/(1 + p^\$)]$ for equation (4.1) and $1 + x_P^{£/\$} = (1 + p^£)/(1 + p^\$)$ for equation (4.2).

Remember: Put the inflation rate of the numerator currency of the FX rate into the numerator term for the inflation rates when using equations (4.1) and (4.2).

Assume that today's APPP spot FX rate for the Swiss franc is 1.60 Sf/$. What will be the spot FX rate a year from now, and what will be the percentage change in the spot FX price of the U.S. dollar, after 5% inflation in Switzerland and 10% inflation in the United States, assuming the RPPP condition holds?

Answer: Using equation (4.1), the time-1 spot FX rate would be (1.60 Sf/$)(1.05/1.10) = 1.527 Sf/$. The RPPP percentage change in the spot FX price of the U.S. dollar is $x^{Sf/\$} = (1.05/1.10) - 1 = -0.0455$.

The RPPP condition is a simple theory of how actual spot FX rates *should* move in a system of flexible FX rates, assuming that the APPP condition is valid. Of course, it is possible for the RPPP condition to hold although the APPP condition does not. Two currencies could be misvalued at both time 0 and time 1, yet the change in the FX rate could be driven exactly by the inflation rate differential, just as the RPPP condition says. Expressed with actual spot FX rates, equation (4.1) would be $X_1^{\$/£} = X_0^{\$/£}(1 + p^\$)/(1 + p^£)$, and equation (4.2) would be $1 + x^{\$/£} = (1 + p^\$)/(1 + p^£)$.

Researchers have found the following empirical results on the RPPP condition using actual spot FX rates: (a) For countries where inflation is high (and thus where goods prices are not sticky), and the FX rate is not controlled by the local government, the RPPP condition is often a reasonably good description of actual spot FX rate movements, because the main factor affecting FX rates is inflation. (b) For other countries, with relatively low inflation, researchers tend to reject the RPPP condition as a description of actual short-term spot FX rate changes, because too many other factors drive FX rates, and because goods prices are sticky. But given that the APPP condition does not fit actual real-world spot FX rates, as we discussed earlier, it should not be surprising if the RPPP condition fails to hold too.

Despite the empirical results that reject the two purchasing power parity (PPP) conditions as a good fit with actual spot FX rates, both conditions are useful factors in FX forecasting. The APPP condition is useful because a deviation from APPP may be forecasted to gradually correct itself. The RPPP condition is useful because inflation rates should be considered in forecasting FX rates. Actual data may not closely fit the two PPP conditions because many other factors also affect FX rates, but the two PPP conditions are fundamentally important.

Fixed FX Rates and Inflation

The Chinese government has controlled the FX rate between the Chinese yuan and the U.S. dollar by not allowing the yuan to be convertible for purposes of capital and portfolio flows. In earlier times, in the *Bretton Woods System*, the FX rates for many freely convertible currencies were held fixed for periods of time by the direct intervention of central banks into the FX market, often in a coordinated fashion among several central banks. The system originated with the Bretton Woods Agreement in 1944. The stability of the pegged FX rates, it was believed, was a means to promote the international trade that would lead to the world's economic recovery after World War II. The Bretton Woods System was maintained until 1973.

The ultimate problem for the Bretton Woods System was that given fixed FX rates, differences in inflation rates led to misvalued currencies in terms of goods prices. Assume that the actual spot FX rate is initially pegged at the APPP spot FX rate, 2.00 $/£. Now let only the United Kingdom experience inflation in goods prices. Assume that the price of a bushel (bu) of wheat there increases from £1.00/bu to £1.60/bu a year later, while the price of a bushel remains at $2.00/bu in the United States. The ILOP condition tells us that the new spot FX rate *should be* ($2.00/bu)/(£1.60/bu) = 1.25 $/£, but the actual FX rate is pegged at 2.00 $/£.

So the ILOP condition no longer holds, once the U.K. price of wheat rises while the actual spot FX rate stays fixed.

At the new wheat prices, unless the actual spot FX rate is allowed to change, the pound and the U.S. dollar are misvalued relative to one another in terms of overseas purchasing power. The pound is overvalued (relative to the U.S. dollar) in terms of overseas purchasing power; correspondingly, the U.S. dollar is undervalued (relative to the pound) in terms of overseas purchasing power. Because the actual spot FX price of the pound (2.00 $/£) is greater than what it should be under the ILOP condition (1.25 $/£), the pound is overvalued, so the U.S. dollar is undervalued.

As we know from previous discussion, a wheat buyer in Britain will now have an incentive to import wheat from the United States. Given the actual pegged FX rate of 2.00 $/£, £1.00 will buy a bushel in the U.S. market, compared with £1.60 to buy a bushel in the UK market. U.S. wheat buyers will likely not import wheat from Britain, since $2.00 buys a bushel in the United States and converts only to £1.00, which buys less than a bushel in the United Kingdom. So trade imbalances follow the currency misvaluation when an FX rate is fixed and inflation rates differ.

Assume that Hong Kong pegs its FX rate in terms of the U.S. dollar at the time when the ILOP condition holds. Hong Kong then experiences higher inflation than the United States.

(a) After the inflation, which currency is overvalued, and which is undervalued?

(b) Which country is likely to experience a trade deficit and which a trade surplus, other things equal?

Answers: (a) After the inflation, the intrinsic FX value of the Hong Kong dollar is lower, but since the actual FX rate is fixed, the Hong Kong dollar is overvalued; thus, the U.S. dollar is undervalued. (b) Hong Kong is likely to be a net importer of U.S. goods and experience a trade deficit, whereas the U.S. will be a net exporter and will have a trade surplus.

An interesting application of this idea is the case of the Chinese yuan. In terms of goods prices, the yuan has for some time been regarded as undervalued relative to the U.S. dollar. But also goods prices in China have been experiencing high inflation. If the inflation persists, given a fixed FX rate, the yuan could eventually become overvalued relative to the U.S. dollar, as the next example demonstrates.

Assume that today the price of a bushel of wheat is ¥14 in China and is $3.75 in the United States. Assume the actual current spot FX rate is 6.60 ¥/$. Assume that over the next five years the inflation rate (in wheat prices) in China will be 15% per year and the inflation rate in the United States will be 2% per year.

(A) Find today's ILOP spot FX rate.

(B) Choose (a), (b), or (c): Today, using the ILOP spot FX rate as the intrinsic FX value, (a) the yuan is undervalued against the U.S. dollar; (b) the yuan is overvalued against the U.S. dollar; (c) the currencies are correctly valued versus each other.

(C) Find the ILOP spot FX rate for 5 years from now.

(D) Assume the spot FX rate is held fixed at today's spot FX rate. Choose (a), (b), or (c): Using the projected inflation rates and the ILOP spot FX rate as the intrinsic FX value, in five years' time, (a) the yuan will be undervalued against the U.S. dollar; (b) the yuan will be overvalued against the U.S. dollar; (c) the currencies will be correctly valued versus each other.

Answers: (A) ¥14/$3.75 = 3.73 ¥/$; (B) (a); (C) 3.73 ¥/$ $(1.15/1.02)^5$ = 6.80 ¥/$; (D) (b).

One can argue that with pegged FX rates there should be pressure on goods prices to change. Although there might be some such pressure, in fact the frictions and the complexity of the real world often make goods prices change very slowly. Thus, the currency misvaluations and trade imbalances may persist for relatively long periods.

We can now understand why the Bretton Woods System of pegged FX rates finally collapsed in the early 1970s. If two countries are experiencing different inflation rates, but FX rates are held fixed by the pegging arrangement, the country with the higher inflation will lose export markets for its goods because its currency is overvalued. With the loss of export markets, the economy suffers and supports fewer jobs. Trade deficits in this case would thus signal potential economic problems. During the period of the Bretton Woods System, countries did follow dissimilar national policies on inflation, and some FX rates became misvalued as a result. Some western European countries had social policies that created high inflation, for example, which with pegged FX rates led to overvalued currencies and trade deficits. At times, these countries tried to stimulate their economies and "import jobs" by resorting to official devaluation, but this tactic was contrary to the design of the Bretton Woods System. Currency speculators compounded the problem by using a country's trade deficit figures to forecast an eventual official devaluation. The speculators would sell the endangered currency before the devaluation, creating further pressure for the central bank to devalue. As long as the central bank delayed the inevitable devaluation, speculators could (and did!) sell the currency and profit at the expense of the central banks that bought when the devaluation inevitably came.

At Bretton Woods, the U.S. dollar was initially pegged at an overvalued FX price to both the German mark and the Japanese yen. The purpose was to help the economies of these two countries, which had been the most devastated by World War II, rebuild their economies by making their goods relatively inexpensive in overseas markets. The plan worked so well that the German and Japanese economies became quite powerful by the late 1960s. (Both countries' economic growth was further enhanced by the absence of military expenditures.) Germany and Japan followed very strict anti-inflation policies to ensure economic recovery and development, and when the United States began to experience higher inflation in the 1960s, the U.S. dollar became even more overvalued relative to the mark and the yen. The economic consequences of misvalued currencies led the participants of the Bretton Woods agreement to dispense with the pegging system in the early 1970s and allow free market floating (flexible) FX rates.

The Euro

After the collapse of the Bretton Woods system, a number of European countries tried to stabilize their FX rates relative to each other under the *European Monetary System*, starting in 1979. The goal of FX stability was intended to facilitate trade within the European Economic Community. The system involved a composite currency, called the *European Currency Unit (ECU)*, consisting of fixed amounts of 12 member currencies. FX rates were pegged relative to the ECU.

But problems and pressures occurred like those that led to the end of the Bretton Woods system. As we said, fixed FX rates do not work well if some countries control inflation and others do not. Other things equal, countries with the higher inflation rates tend to want to devalue their currency when it gets overvalued. This defeats the purpose of the pegged FX system. By 1992, the drive for monetary stability led to the *Maastricht Treaty*, in which a number of European nations established the European Central Bank (ECB) and agreed to use a single currency, the euro. This monetary unification was designed to overcome the problems of pegged FX rates that countries can devalue at almost any time. In the years just before the introduction of the euro, it was essential to stabilize the FX rates of the existing European currencies. The reason was that the national currencies had to be converted into the euro at a fixed FX rate. To prevent misvaluations, countries participating in the euro had to harmonize their economic policies in terms of growth, inflation rate, money supply, and so forth. In 1999, the euro was launched as an electronic currency and finally, in 2002, national currencies were replaced with the euro as legal tender. Denmark, Sweden, and the United Kingdom were the only members of the European Economic Community that did not join the euro. For the members that did join the euro, the uncertainty and transaction costs of exchanging currencies with each other has been reduced, encouraging trade and economic prosperity.

The euro began to experience problems when some countries tried to diverge from the harmonized economic policies. The most notable example is Greece, but Italy, Portugal, and Spain have also had economic problems that have created strains on the euro arrangement.

Currency Boards and Dollarization

Not all FX pegging is doomed. A number of smaller countries with stable economies maintain FX rates that are pegged to a major hard currency. The Hong Kong dollar (HK$) is an example of a currency that has been tied to the U.S. dollar for many years. The method used by Hong Kong is called a *currency board*. A currency board has four tenets: (a) to prohibit the central bank from printing money that is not backed by FX reserves of hard foreign currencies; (b) to permit the country's currency to be freely redeemed on demand for hard-currency FX reserves, a feature called *free convertibility*; (c) to peg that currency's FX price to a hard currency, often the currency of the major trading partner; and (d) to require the government to maintain responsible economic policies.

Argentina successfully operated a currency board plan for a while in the 1990s, but it gave way in early 2002 amidst economic crisis. Argentina had been plagued by high inflation until 1991. In one month in 1989, goods prices in Argentina rose by nearly 2,300%. This kind of inflation caused currency depreciation and discouraged investment. With the currency board plan, inflation was under control by 1992, and Argentina's economy got on track. But the plan failed in the fourth tenet, to require the government to maintain responsible economic policies. By 2002, the inability of the country's politicians to curb government spending and reform labor laws had created political and economic chaos.

Dollarization is the replacement of local currency with the U.S. dollar. It may seem like a large loss in prestige for a country to give up its own currency, but this may be acceptable when the alternative is monetary chaos. Ecuador and El Salvador, for example, have dollarized. Dollarization is a legalization of the natural use of a hard currency as a store of value in soft-currency countries, which is quite frequent.

Adjusted APPP

Take a look at which currencies are overvalued and which are undervalued in Exhibit 3.1. You will see that overvalued currencies often belong to countries that are more affluent, whereas the undervalued currencies tend to belong to less developed economies. This observed pattern is consistent with an economic principle called the *Balassa–Samuelson effect*, which has three features: (a) Nontraded goods (e.g., "haircuts") for two economies do not have the same price ratio as tradable goods; the more developed economy will have higher relative prices for nontraded goods. (b) The ILOP condition holds for tradable goods. (c) Using the APPP standard of intrinsic FX value, the more developed economy will appear to have an overvalued currency, and the less-developed economy will appear to have an undervalued currency, even if the actual FX rate is correctly valued by the ILOP condition.

For example, say the price of a bushel of wheat (a tradable commodity) in the United States is $10 per bushel and in Mexico is Pe140 per bushel. Thus, given that the ILOP condition holds for wheat, the actual spot FX rate, $X^{Pe/\$}$, would be 14 Pe/$. Next assume the price of a haircut in the United States is $10, and in Mexico is Pe100. So relative to wheat, haircuts are more expensive in the United States than in Mexico. Now consider a "basket" of the two consumption goods. A basket of one bushel of wheat and one haircut costs $20 in the United States and costs Pe240 in Mexico. Using the APPP idea of a basket of consumption goods as the basis for intrinsic FX value, the APPP FX rate is Pe240/$20 = 12 Pe/$. At the actual FX rate of 14 Pe/$, the U.S. dollar appears overvalued relative to the Mexican peso, and the Mexican peso appears undervalued relative to the U.S. dollar, compared with the APPP FX rate of 12 Pe/$.

As we said, higher relative prices of nontraded goods are typically found in more developed economies. One reason is that wage rates and other labor costs are lower in less-developed countries, and many nontraded goods are service-oriented and labor intensive. Thus, the Balassa–Samuelson effect is generally interpreted to mean that more developed economies will appear to have overvalued currencies based on the APPP standard of FX value, due to relatively high prices for nontraded goods, even if the actual FX rate is correctly valued under the ILOP condition for prices of the tradable goods. So the problem is that the APPP approach may not be able to tell us whether a currency is really misvalued or not. Put another way, we cannot tell from Exhibit 3.1 whether the FX rates are really misvalued, after adjusting for the Balassa–Samuelson effect.

To build the Balassa–Samuelson effect into the purchasing power analysis, the *Economist* creates a "line-of-best-fit" through a scatter plot for the Big Mac prices in U.S. dollars (*Y*-axis) and GDP per capita in U.S. dollars (*X*-axis). An economy's "line-of-best-fit" Big Mac price is the assumed basis of the intrinsic FX value. Figure 4.2 depicts this analysis using data for January 31, 2013. A plot above (below) the horizontal line at $4.37 is overvalued (undervalued) by the APPP standard. A plot above (below) the "line-of-best-fit" is overvalued (undervalued) by the adjusted APPP standard.

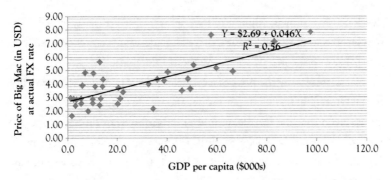

Figure 4.2. Adjusted Big Mac index.

The graph in Figure 4.2 corresponds to the data in Exhibit 4.1. The first and second columns in Exhibit 4.1 repeat data in Exhibit 3.1 for the raw index. The third column shows GDP per capita (in thousands), expressed in U.S. dollars. The fourth column contains the adjusted Big Mac price. The fifth column shows the percentage currency misvaluation, by comparing the actual Big Mac price (in the first column) to the adjusted Big Mac price (in the fourth column). In Exhibit 4.1, the "line-of-best-fit" is $Y = 2.69 + 0.046X$, where Y is the adjusted Big Mac price in U.S. dollars and X is GDP per capita (in thousands of U.S. dollars). (Data for Figure 4.2 and Exhibit 4.1 are from the site: http://www. economist.com/content/big-mac-index.)

For example, with the Euro area's $40,140 in GDP per capita (in U.S. dollars), the adjusted Big Mac price should be $2.69 + 0.046(40.14) = $4.54, roughly the number in Exhibit 4.1. Thus using equation (3.3), the "line-of-best-fit" says the euro *should be* misvalued by $4.54/$4.37 − 1 = 0.0389, or 3.89% overvalued, relative to the APPP spot FX rate. Since the APPP spot FX rate is 1.217 $/€ (see Exhibit 3.1), the adjusted APPP spot FX rate is (1.217 $/€)(1.0389) = 1.264 $/€. Given the actual FX rate of 1.36 $/€ (see Exhibit 3.1), the percentage misvaluation of the euro relative to the adjusted APPP intrinsic spot FX rate is (1.36 $/€)/(1.264 $/€) − 1 = 0.076, or a 7.6% euro overvaluation. A short-cut, analogous to equation (3.3), is to find the percentage that the actual Euro area Big Mac price (in U.S. dollars), $4.88, differs from the adjusted Big Mac price implied by the "line-of-best-fit," $4.54: $4.88/$4.54 − 1 = 0.075, or 7.5% overvaluation (difference due to rounding). So the actual spot FX price of the euro is about 7.5% overvalued relative to adjusted APPP intrinsic spot FX rate.

Exhibit 4.1. Big Mac Adjusted PPP Index

Country	Big Mac price($)	Raw % FX misvalue	GDP per cap ($000s)	Adj Mac price($)	Adj % FX misvalue
United States	4.37		48.33		
Argentina	3.82	−12.58	10.96	3.19	19.65
Australia	4.90	12.21	66.37	5.73	−14.43
Brazil	5.64	29.22	12.79	3.27	72.35
Britain	4.25	−2.73	38.81	4.47	−4.87
Canada	5.39	23.51	50.50	5.00	7.88
Chile	4.35	−0.50	14.40	3.35	29.77
China	2.57	−41.10	5.42	2.94	−12.43
Colombia	4.85	11.05	7.11	3.01	60.87
Czech Republic	3.72	−14.77	20.44	3.62	2.69
Denmark	5.18	18.69	59.71	5.42	−4.40
Egypt	2.39	−45.20	2.93	2.82	−15.24
Euro area	4.88	11.69	40.14	4.53	7.77
Hong Kong	2.19	−49.83	34.26	4.26	−48.54
Hungary	3.82	−12.61	14.05	3.33	14.53
India	1.67	−61.83	1.51	2.76	−39.58
Indonesia	2.86	−34.51	3.51	2.85	0.36
Israel	4.00	−8.40	32.35	4.17	−4.07
Japan	3.51	−19.54	45.87	4.79	−26.62
Malaysia	2.58	−40.96	10.09	3.15	−18.16
Mexico	2.90	−33.49	10.15	3.15	−7.90
New Zealand	4.32	−0.98	35.97	4.34	−0.26
Norway	7.84	79.56	97.61	7.16	9.58
Pakistan	2.97	−32.01	1.20	2.74	8.20
Peru	3.91	−10.54	5.90	2.96	32.01
Philippines	2.91	−33.45	2.35	2.80	3.92
Poland	2.94	−32.61	13.47	3.31	−10.97
Russia	2.43	−44.46	12.99	3.28	−26.14
Saudi Arabia	2.93	−32.84	21.20	3.66	−19.85
Singapore	3.64	−16.56	49.27	4.94	−26.30

(Continued)

Exhibit 4.1. Big Mac Adjusted PPP Index (Continued)

Country	Big Mac price($)	Raw % FX misvalue	GDP per cap ($000s)	Adj Mac price($)	Adj % FX misvalue
South Africa	2.03	−53.61	8.08	3.06	−33.77
South Korea	3.41	−21.95	22.42	3.72	−8.26
Sweden	7.62	74.54	57.64	5.33	43.09
Switzerland	7.12	63.14	83.07	6.49	9.76
Taiwan	2.54	−41.79	20.08	3.61	−29.55
Thailand	2.92	−33.05	5.40	2.94	−0.42
Turkey	4.78	9.39	10.36	3.16	51.01

This percentage is approximately as shown in the fifth column of Exhibit 4.1 (difference due to rounding).

In Chapter 3, we saw an undervaluation of the Chinese yuan by 41.2% relative to the APPP intrinsic spot FX rate using the Big Mac index. The last column in Exhibit 4.1 says that the Chinese yuan is undervalued by only 12.43% relative to the adjusted APPP intrinsic spot FX rate based on Big Mac prices, GDP, and the "line-of-best fit."

(a) Use the "line-of-best-fit" equation to verify that the adjusted Chinese Big Mac price is approximately $2.94 (as shown in the fourth column).

(b) Given the actual and APPP spot FX rates for the yuan, 6.22 ¥/$ and 3.66 ¥/$ (see Exhibit 3.1), find the adjusted APPP spot FX rate, and verify that the yuan is undervalued by approximately 12.43%, adjusted for GDP.

(c) Verify that the Chinese yuan is undervalued by approximately 12.43% using the short-cut approach with the Chinese actual Big Mac price in US dollars (first column) and the adjusted Chinese Big Mac price in US dollars (fourth column).

Answers: (a) $2.69 + 0.046(5.42) = $2.94; (b) The "line-of-best-fit" says the yuan should be misvalued by $2.94/$4.37 − 1 = −0.327, or 32.7% undervalued, relative to the APPP spot FX rate. The adjusted APPP spot FX rate in $/¥ is thus (1/(3.66 ¥/$))(1 − 0.327) = 0.1839 $/¥, which is 5.438 ¥/$. Given the actual spot FX rate of 6.22 ¥/$, the

Exhibit 4.2. OECD Absolute Purchasing Power Parity (Raw and Adjusted)

Country	Basket price ($)	GDP per cap ($000s)	Adj Basket price ($)	Adj % FX misvalue
Australia	167	66.371	152.95	9.18
Britain	119	38.811	114.98	3.50
Canada	130	50.496	131.08	−0.82
Chile	80	14.403	81.34	−1.65
Czech Republic	81	20.436	89.65	−9.65
Denmark	154	59.709	143.77	7.11
Hungary	70	14.050	80.85	−13.43
Israel	119	32.351	106.07	12.19
Japan	136	45.870	124.70	9.06
Mexico	73	10.146	75.48	−3.28
New Zealand	134	35.973	111.06	20.65
Norway	175	97.607	196.00	−10.71
Poland	65	13.469	80.05	−18.81
South Korea	86	22.424	92.39	−6.92
Sweden	140	57.638	140.92	−0.65
Switzerland	169	83.073	175.97	−3.96
Turkey	75	10.363	75.77	−1.02

percentage misvaluation of the yuan relative to the adjusted APPP intrinsic spot FX rate is equal to $(1/(6.22 \ ¥/\$))/(0.1839 \ \$/¥) - 1 = -0.126$, or a 12.6% undervaluation of the yuan. (c) $\$2.57/\$2.94 - 1 = -0.126$, a 12.6% undervaluation of the yuan, slightly different from -12.43% in Exhibit 4.1 due to rounding.

Although not as visible as the Big Mac approach to APPP, the Organization for Economic Cooperation and Development (OECD) computes some APPP FX rate estimates using broad consumption baskets, as we said earlier. The OECD approach may also be adjusted for the Balassa–Samuelson effect. Exhibit 4.2 shows some data for the OECD approach to APPP, from the Web site: http://www.oecd.org/std/prices-ppp/purchasingpowerparitiespppsdata.htm. The first column shows the

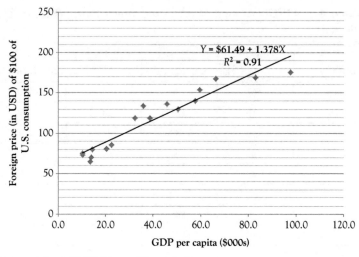

Figure 4.3. OECD "*line-of-best-fit.*"

price of an economy's consumption basket (in U.S. dollars) of $100 spent on the same basket in the United States. The price of such a basket in Australia is $167. So the first column tells us the FX misvaluation based on the raw APPP for the basket. Specifically, the Australian dollar is 67% overvalued. The Chilean peso is 20% undervalued, and so forth. The second column of Exhibit 4.2 shows GDP per capita.

The "line-of-best-fit" is found by linear regression of the first column on the second column; approximately, the "line-of-best-fit" equation is $Y = \$61.49 + 1.378X$, where Y is the economy's price of the consumption basket (in U.S. dollars) and X is the economy's GDP per capita. This "line-of-best-fit" is shown in Figure 4.3. The third column of Exhibit 4.2, the adjusted basket price, shows the economy's "line-of-best-fit" consumption basket price (in U.S. dollars). For Australia, the adjusted basket price is $61.49 + 1.378(66.371) = \$152.95$. The percentage currency misvaluation is gauged by taking the percentage of the actual basket price (first column) relative to the adjusted basket price (third column). For the Australian dollar, the calculation is $167/\$152.95 - 1 = 0.0918$, or 9.18%. The percentage misvaluation, based on the adjusted approach to APPP, is shown in the fourth column. As we see, the Australian dollar is overvalued by only 9.18% when the Balassa–Samuelson effect is considered.

The OECD data in Exhibit 4.2 says that the Norwegian krone is over-valued by 75% based on raw APPP, but is undervalued by 10.71% based on adjusted APPP.

(a) Verify the adjusted Norwegian price of $100 of U.S. consumption is $196 (as shown in the third column) using the OECD "line-of-best-fit" equation.

(b) Verify the undervaluation of the Norwegian krone is approximately 10.71% using the Norwegian actual basket price in U.S. dollars (first column) and the adjusted Norwegian basket price in U.S. dollars (third column).

Answers: (a) $61.49 + 1.378(97.607) = $196; (b) $175/$196 − 1 = −0.1071, a 10.71% undervaluation of the Norwegian krone.

Whether you prefer to use Big Macs or the OECD basket, or some other standard, the raw APPP FX rate gives one estimate of the intrinsic FX rate. The empirical "line-of-best-fit" reflects another estimate of the intrinsic FX rate, after adjusting for the Balassa–Samuelson effect. Currencies of low GDP countries may be undervalued relative to the APPP condition, but may not be undervalued relative to the estimated "line-of-best-fit." Similarly, currencies of high GDP countries tend to be overvalued relative to the raw APPP condition, but may not be overvalued relative to the estimated "line-of-best-fit." We can think of the raw APPP condition as giving an estimate of the *long-run* intrinsic FX rate, whereas the "line-of-best-fit" gives an estimate of the *medium-run* intrinsic FX rate.

Note also that there are other reasons why the APPP condition may not hold, even after adjusting for the Balassa–Samuelson effect. One of these reasons is imperfect competition, where a product's price will depend on local conditions and the difficulty in reselling products across borders. For example, because of differences in safety and pollution standards, as well as warranty restrictions, it is difficult for individuals to resell automobiles across borders.

Summary Action Points

- The RPPP condition is a theoretical relationship between inflation rates and changes in intrinsic spot FX rates based on the APPP condition.

- Actual spot FX rate changes often deviate from the RPPP condition because other factors besides inflation are at work.
- Different national economic policies that affect inflation will lead to FX misvaluations, and thus possible trade imbalances, if FX rates are controlled. This problem led to the post-Bretton Woods floating FX rate regime in the international markets, and helped the evolution of the euro as the one currency of many European countries.
- The Balassa–Samuelson effect implies that intrinsic FX rates *should* differ from the APPP FX rates. A high-GDP country should have an overvalued currency and a low-GDP country should have an undervalued currency, relative to the APPP condition. Better estimates of intrinsic FX values are based on an adjusted APPP condition, which an empirical "line-of-best-fit" between goods prices based on actual FX rates and GDP per capita.
- Models of intrinsic FX value are useful even if they don't "fit" the data, because we get an idea of whether a currency is misvalued and may be due for a correction.

Glossary

Adjusted APPP FX rate: The intrinsic FX rate after adjusting the APPP intrinsic FX rate for a country's GDP per capita, based on the Balassa–Samuelson effect and an empirical "line-of-best-fit."

Balassa–Samuelson effect: A theory that actual FX rates appear misvalued by the APPP condition, even if correctly valued by the ILOP condition.

Bretton Woods system: The international system from 1944 to 1973 in which many nations agreed to maintain stable, or pegged, FX rates.

Currency board: A monetary authority that stabilizes a currency by backing it with hard-currency reserves.

Dollarization: The replacement of a national currency with the U.S. dollar.

ECB: European Central Bank.

European currency unit (ECU): A unit of account that was used before the euro; it was a composite of 12 European currencies.

Line-of-best-fit: An empirical relationship between spot FX values and GDP per capita that gauges adjusted APPP intrinsic FX rates.

Maastricht Treaty: The agreement in 1992 by a number of European nations that established the European Central Bank (ECB) and the use a single currency, the euro.

Mercantilism: A national strategy to increase wealth at the expense of another country through international trade.

Relative purchasing power parity (RPPP): A theory concept describing how FX rates should change according to inflation rates.

Discussion Questions

1. Explain the difference between the RPPP condition and the APPP condition.
2. Explain why the pegged FX rates of the Bretton Woods system gave way to flexible (floating) rates.
3. Explain the Balassa–Samuelson effect.
4. Explain the adjusted APPP condition and the "line-of-best-fit."

Problems

1. Assume the price of a Big Mac is €2.50 in Europe and is $3.00 in the United States. The actual spot FX rate is 1.35 $/€. Over the next year the inflation rate (in goods prices) in Europe is 4% and in the United States is 3%. Assume that Big Mac prices are the benchmark for intrinsic FX value. (A) Find the time-0 APPP spot FX rate; (B) Choose (a), (b), or (c): At time 0, (a) the U.S. dollar is undervalued against the euro; (b) the U.S. dollar overvalued against the euro; (c) cannot tell if the currencies are misvalued. (C) Find the APPP spot FX rate a year from now. (D) You forecast that the actual spot FX rate a year from now will be the APPP spot FX rate. What is your forecasted percentage change in the actual spot FX price of the euro?

2. At time 0, the yen price of a bushel of wheat is ¥150 and the U.S. dollar price of a bushel of wheat is $1. Assume that the actual spot FX rate at time 0 is $X_0^{¥/\$} = 150$ ¥/$. (Thus, in purchasing power terms, the spot FX rate is correctly valued relative to wheat at time 0.) Now assume that inflation is zero in both countries and that the actual time-1 spot FX rate is $X_1^{¥/\$} = 120$ ¥/$. Choose (a), (b), or (c): In terms of purchasing power, at time 1 there is (a) an overvalued yen and an undervalued U.S. dollar, (b) an overvalued U.S. dollar and an undervalued yen, or (c) neither.

3. Let the inflation rate between time 0 and time 1 be 30% in Britain and 10% in the United States. According to the RPPP condition, what should be the percentage change between the time-0 and time-1 spot FX prices of the British pound?

4. Assume the time-0 APPP spot FX rate is 1.60 $/£. Let the inflation rate between time 0 and time 1 be 30% in Britain and 10% in the United States. According to the RPPP condition, what should be the time-1 spot FX rate?

5. Assume that the APPP condition is the correct model of intrinsic FX value. Suppose that at time 0, the actual spot FX rate of 1.60 $/£ represents the correct FX value of the pound. Let the inflation rate in the United Kingdom between time 0 and time 1 be 30%, while U.S. goods prices drop by 10%. If the actual spot FX rate goes from 1.60 $/£ to 1.40 $/£ during this same time period, (a) the pound became overvalued relative to the U.S. dollar, (b) the U.S. dollar became overvalued relative to the pound, or (c) neither misvaluation occurred?

6. At time 0, the price of a bushel of wheat is ¥150 in Japan and $1 in the United States. The actual spot FX rate at time 0 is $X_0^{¥/\$} = 150$ ¥/$. The inflation rate in Japan is 5% per year, whereas the inflation rate is 10% per year in the United States. Now assume that the spot FX rate is fixed, so that the actual time-1 spot FX rate is $X_1^{¥/\$} = 150$ ¥/$. (A) What would the RPPP condition say that the time-1 spot FX rate should be, in conventional European terms? (B) In terms of purchasing power at time 1, is there (a) an overvalued yen and an undervalued U.S. dollar, (b) an overvalued U.S. dollar and an undervalued yen, or (c) neither?

7. Assume that today the price of a bushel of wheat is ¥18 in China and is $3.00 in the United States. Assume the actual current spot FX rate is 6.60 ¥/$. Assume that over the next year the inflation rate (in wheat prices) in China will be 15% and the inflation rate in the United States will be 2%. Assume the actual spot FX rate is held fixed at today's spot FX rate.

(A) Circle (a), (b), or (c), and justify your answer: Today, using the ILOP spot FX rate as the intrinsic FX value, (a) the yuan is under-valued against the U.S. dollar; (b) the yuan is overvalued against the U.S. dollar; (c) the currencies are correctly valued versus each other.

(B) Circle (a), (b), or (c), and explain your answer: Using the projected inflation rates and the ILOP spot FX rate as the intrinsic FX rate, at time 1: (a) the yuan will be undervalued; (b) the yuan will be overvalued; (c) the yuan will be correctly valued.

8. The price of a Big Mac is €2.00 in Europe and is $2.50 in the United States. The actual spot FX rate is 1.50 $/€. Using the adjusted APPP approach based on GDP per capita, the "line-of-best-fit" says that the euro should be overvalued by 40%.

(A) What is the intrinsically correct spot FX rate, given the "line-of-best-fit"?

(B) Circle (a), (b), or (c), and briefly justify your answer: Based on the "line-of-best-fit" in the adjusted Big Mac approach: (a) The U.S. dollar is undervalued against the euro; (b) the U.S. dollar overvalued against the euro; (c) the currencies are not misvalued.

9. The last column in Exhibit 4.1 says that the Brazilian real is overvalued by 72.35%. (a) Use the "line-of-best-fit" equation to verify that the adjusted Brazilian Big Mac price (in U.S. dollars) is approximately $3.27 (as in the fourth column). (b) Verify that the overvaluation of the Brazilian real is approximately 72.35% using the Brazilian actual Big Mac price in U.S. dollars (first column) and the adjusted Brazilian Big Mac price in U.S. dollars (fourth column).

10. The OECD data in Exhibit 4.2 says that the Turkish lira is undervalued by 25% based on raw APPP, but is undervalued by only 1.02% based on adjusted APPP. (a) Verify that in U.S. dollars, the adjusted Turkish price of $100 of U.S. consumption is $75.77 (as shown in the third column) using the OECD "line-of-best-fit" equation. (b) Verify the undervaluation of the Turkish lira is approximately 1.02% using the Turkish actual basket price in U.S. dollars (first column) and the adjusted Turkish basket price in U.S. dollars (third column).

Answers to Problems

1. (A) The APPP spot FX rate is 1.20 $/€;

(B) (a) The euro is currently overvalued, and the U.S. dollar is undervalued;

(C) A year from now, the APPP spot FX rate should be (1.20 $/€) (1.03/1.04) = 1.19 $/€;

(D) (1.19 $/€)/(1.35 $/€) − 1 = −0.12, or −12%

2. (a) Because the parity FX rate is 150 ¥/$ at time 0, and since there is no inflation for either country, equation (4.4) tells us that the parity FX rate at time 1 will be 150 ¥/$(1.00/1.00) = 150 ¥/$. Because the actual FX rate at time 1 of 120 ¥/$ is below the parity rate, the U.S. dollar is undervalued relative to the yen, and the yen is overvalued relative to the U.S. dollar.

3. Using equation (4.2), we get 1.10/1.30 − 1 = −0.154, or −15.4%.

4. 1.60 $/£(1.10/1.30) = 1.35 $/£

5. (a) The APPP spot FX rate at time 1 is 1.60 $/£(1 − 0.10)/(1.30) = 1.11 $/£. Because the actual FX rate is higher than the APPP FX rate, the British pound is overvalued.

6. (A) 150 ¥/$(1.05/1.10) = 143.18 ¥/$;

   (B) (b)

7. (A) ¥18/$3 = 6 ¥/$; (a)

   (B) (b) the yuan will be overvalued; 6 ¥/$(1.15/1.02) = 6.76 ¥/$

8. (A) 1.40($2.50/€2.00) = 1.75 $/€

   (B) (b) The U.S. dollar is overvalued against the euro

9. (a) $2.69 + 0.046(12.79) = $3.278;

   (b) $5.64/$3.278 − 1 = 0.7204, a 72.04% overvaluation of the Brazilian real, slightly different from 72.35% due to rounding.

10. (a) $61.49 + 1.378(10.363) = $75.77;

    (b) $75/$75.77 − 1 = −0.0102, a 1.02% undervaluation of the Turkish lira.

CHAPTER 5

Interest Rates
and Foreign Exchange

In addition to the purchasing power approach, we can view intrinsic foreign exchange (FX) rates in terms of financial assets, particularly in terms of interest rates. This chapter introduces the role of interest rates in intrinsic FX valuation. As we said, managers need to understand when an FX rate is misvalued to optimize risk management, capital structure, and capital investment decisions.

An intrinsic FX rate that is consistent with valuation in financial markets may be thought of as a *short-run intrinsic FX rate*. Note that there can simultaneously be both a long-run (goods market) intrinsic spot FX rate and a short-run (financial market) intrinsic spot FX rate. As we'll see, these two intrinsic spot FX rates do not have to be equal to each other, nor does the actual spot FX rate have to be equal to either intrinsic spot FX rate.

The London Interbank Offer Rate

Some years ago, banks generally accepted customers' deposits denominated only in the currency of the country in which the bank was domiciled. The situation is different now. Deposit and loan services in major currencies frequently take place outside the geographic area in which a given currency is legal tender, owing to the *eurodollar* concept, which originated in the 1950s. Communist governments, needing U.S. dollars for international trade because their own currencies were not acceptable, feared a potential freeze of their U.S. dollar deposits held at U.S. banks or their foreign subsidiaries. They instead asked some European banks, especially ones in London, to hold their U.S. dollar deposits. The banks realized there was nothing to stop them from denominating a deposit in U.S. dollars, promising to pay interest in U.S. dollars, and then re-lending the deposited U.S. dollars elsewhere (outside the United States) at a higher rate of interest.

Regular business customers accepted this idea. By the 1960s, it had become common for non-U.S. banks to conduct banking services in U.S. dollars. As the practice originated in Europe, the term *eurodollar* was coined. Later, as U.S. dollar deposits and loans occurred elsewhere, particularly in Asia, the term eurodollar persisted and became the general term used for any U.S. dollar denominated deposit or loan outside the United States.

The eurodollar concept was extended to euroyen, eurosterling, euro-Swiss francs, and so forth. In general, the term *eurocurrency* applies to any time deposit or time loan outside the country of the particular currency. Currently, the *eurocurrency market* involves globally traded, zero coupon time deposits and time loans in various currencies. Global competition between banks assures that there is, more or less, one global interest rate for each currency (for a given horizon and credit rating). In other words, at a given bank in any country, an AAA-rated borrower of yen from France would pay (more or less) the same interest rate as an AAA-rated borrower of yen from Korea. The eurocurrency market has substantial liquidity and is thoroughly integrated with the FX market. The term "eurocurrency market" may be a little misleading, because the deposits and loans are not necessarily denominated in euros or any other European currency.

Suppose a company in any country wants to borrow yen for a year. A company with a sufficient line of credit with a bank makes a simple call to the banker, and the deal is almost instantaneous. The bank, practically simultaneously, can electronically shop the wholesale interbank market. If a Swiss bank quotes the best one-year borrowing rate for yen, the company's bank can instantaneously borrow the yen from the Swiss bank and then re-lend them to the retail customer at a markup.

Despite the global nature of the eurocurrency market, its geographic center is, by size and tradition, London. Hence, London banks' eurocurrency quotes are surveyed as a method for obtaining the representative focus of the market. The average of the borrowing or "offer" rate is the London Interbank Offer Rate (LIBOR). There is a different LIBOR rate for each currency and time to maturity. There is a three-month yen LIBOR, a one-year Swiss franc LIBOR, and so forth. Maturities of one week, three months, six months, nine months, and one year are the most popular in the eurocurrency market, but markets in some eurocurrencies are active for other maturities, including two-year, three-year, five-year, and higher.

To obtain real-time euromarket interest rates, you need a service such as Bloomberg or Reuters, which costs money. Exhibit 5.1 shows some one-year LIBOR rates for various currencies on five dates: February 18, 2013; May 31, 2011; June 29, 2007; November 17, 2003; and August 9, 2002.

Carry Trades

There is a common strategy called a *currency carry trade*, or often simply a *carry trade*. In this trade, a speculator will borrow in a low interest rate currency, spot FX the loan proceeds into a high interest rate currency, and then deposit at the high interest rate.

Carry Trade:
- Borrow Low Interest Rate Currency
- Spot FX to the High Interest Rate Currency
- Deposit in High Interest Rate Currency

Exhibit 5.1. One-year LIBOR (%): Selected Dates

	2/18/13[a]	5/31/11[b]	6/29/07[b]	11/17/03[b]	8/09/02[b]
EUR (Euro)	0.47	2.11	4.52	2.35	3.39
GBP (Sterling)	0.96	1.59	6.32	4.45	4.10
AUD (Australian dollar)	3.57	5.67	6.76	5.80	5.03
CHF (Swiss franc)	0.28	0.54	3.05	0.55	1.05
CAD (Canadian dollar)	1.86	1.91	4.84	2.97	2.96
USD (US dollar)	0.76	0.73	5.45	1.43	1.85
JPY (Japanese yen)	0.47	0.56	0.99	0.09	0.09
NZD (New Zealand)	3.34				
SEK (Swedish krone)	1.74				
DKK (Danish krone)	0.71				

Sources:
[a]http://www.global-rates.com/interest-rates/libor/libor.aspx
[b]British Bankers Association (http://www.bbalibor.com/rates/historical).

The trader lays out no capital for a carry trade, but hopes to profit if the higher interest rate currency does not depreciate by too much relative to the lower interest rate currency. Carry trades are especially profitable if the higher interest rate currency appreciates relative to the lower interest rate currency. Because the carry trade itself represents a demand for the higher interest rate currency, carry traders hope that other carry traders will come along after them, with further buying of the higher interest rate currency, helping to further push up the spot FX price of the high interest currency.

Before the financial crisis of 2008, a number of hedge funds had significant carry trade positions, with borrowing typically in yen and investing often in Australian dollars, New Zealand dollars, and euros. Indeed, by early 2007, about $1 trillion was staked on the carry trade, according to the *Economist*. The continued accumulation of these carry trade positions resulted in an appreciating A$, NZ$, and euro, and a depreciating yen. So these carry trade positions were profitable, by getting the interest rate spread plus FX movements in a favorable direction. But once the financial crisis got into full swing, the carry traders began to unwind (liquidate) their positions, spot FXing the proceeds into yen, and using the yen proceeds to pay off the yen loans. This unwinding caused the FX price of the yen to rise and the FX price of the A$, NZ$, and euro to fall during the crisis. Then *all* the carry traders began to unwind their positions for fear of further depreciation in the FX price of the A$, NZ$, and euro relative to the yen. Of course, the more carry trade positions that were liquidated, the more the A$, NZ$, and euro dropped and the more the yen rose. From April to November in 2008, the euro depreciated from almost 1.60 $/€ to nearly 1.25 $/€. Over the same time period, the yen appreciated from nearly 105 ¥/$ to around 88 ¥/$.

A Carry Trade Exchange Traded Fund

Deutsche Bank sponsored an exchange traded fund (ETF), which allows individual investors to participate in the carry trade strategy. Basically the fund borrows funds in low interest rate currencies and deposits the funds in high interest rate currencies. The ETF is named the DB G10 Currency Harvest Fund, with ticker symbol DBV. A chart for DBV is shown below.

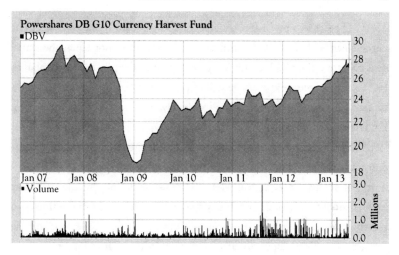

Uncovered Interest Rate Parity

There is a theory that if spot FX rates are correctly valued, carry traders should not expect to earn a profit. The theory is called the *Uncovered Interest Rate Parity (UIRP)* condition. According to the UIRP theory, the current spot FX rate should be aligned with interest rates and the expected future spot FX rate. Just as the absolute purchasing power parity (APPP) condition provides a measure of intrinsic FX value based on goods markets, so the UIRP theory provides a measure of intrinsic FX value based on financial markets.

The UIRP condition is shown in equation (5.1), where r^{Sf} and $r^{\$}$ represent the annualized interest rate on a zero-coupon eurocurrency instrument in Swiss francs and U.S. dollars, respectively, between now and time N. The UIRP condition is also sometimes called the *International Fisher equation* or the *Fisher open equation*, after the economist Irving Fisher.

Uncovered Interest Rate Parity

$$E(X_N^{Sf/\$}) = X_{U0}^{Sf/\$}[(1 + r^{Sf})/(1 + r^{\$})]^N \qquad (5.1)$$

On the left-hand side of the equality in equation (5.1) is the *expected* future spot FX rate at time N, $E(X_N^{Sf/\$})$. On the right side of the equality is the current spot FX rate that *should* prevail if the UIRP condition holds,

$X_{U0}{}^{Sf/\$}$. The subscript U denotes that the spot FX rate is one that would be observed only if the UIRP condition holds, and does not equal the actual spot FX rate if the UIRP condition does not hold. Despite the way equation (5.1) is set up, the unknown we will often want to find is the time-0 intrinsic spot FX rate, $X_{U0}{}^{Sf/\$}$, on the right side, given a forecast of the future spot FX rate on the left side, $E(X_N{}^{Sf/\$})$.

The UIRP condition in equation (5.1) is set up this way to be consistent with the way that the relative purchasing power parity (RPPP) condition is set up in equation (4.1). That is, with the "future" FX rate isolated on the left side, and today's spot FX rate on the right side, you put the interest rate of the "numerator" currency in the numerator and the interest rate of the "denominator" currency in the denominator.

For a numerical example, assume $N = 1$, $r^{Sf} = 0.04$, $r^{\$} = 0.06$, and $E(X_1{}^{Sf/\$}) = 1.57$ Sf/\$. Plug these numbers where they belong in equation (5.1), and then rearrange to solve for the unknown, $X_{U0}{}^{Sf/\$}$. Thus the UIRP condition, equation (5.1), says that today's spot FX rate should be $X_{U0}{}^{Sf/\$} = 1.60$ Sf/\$. This is the intrinsic spot FX rate, given the forecasted future spot FX rate of 1.57 Sf/\$ and that the UIRP condition holds. Figure 5.1 lays out the details of this example.

The one-year interest rate in U.S. dollars is 7% and in yen is 2%. The expected spot FX for a year from now is 104 ¥/\$. What is the intrinsic spot FX rate, given the UIRP condition?

Answer: You want to find $X_{U0}{}^{¥/\$}$ such that $E(X_1{}^{¥/\$}) = 104$ ¥/\$ $= X_{U0}{}^{¥/\$}$ $[(1 + r^{¥})/(1 + r^{\$})] = X_{U0}{}^{¥/\$}(1.02/1.07)$. Thus, $X_{U0}{}^{¥/\$} = 109.10$ ¥/\$.

Of course, we need to address the question, "Where does the forecasted spot FX rate come from?" Such a forecast should be based on an analysis of fundamental economic variables. One possibility is to use a long-run forecast, such as a forecasted APPP FX rate, as you will see done in the next section. For a shorter horizon, which we use in this section for simplicity, a corporate manager will often use a forecast from a bank's research/economic department, or maybe an average of several bank forecasts. Examples of bank forecasts are discussed in the box titled "Bank FX Forecasts: 2004 and 2012."

	Date		
	0		1
Currency			
U.S. dollars	$1	$x\,(1 + 0.06)$	$= \$1.06$
	$X_{U0}^{Sf/\$} = 1.60\ Sf/\$$		$E(X_1^{Sf/\$}) = X_{U0}^{Sf/\$}(1 + r^{Sf})/(1 + r^{\$})$ $1.57\ Sf/\$ = \mathbf{1.60}\ Sf/\$(1.04/1.06)$
Swiss francs	Sf 1.60	$x\,(1 + 0.04)$	$= Sf\ 1.664$

Figure 5.1. Uncovered interest rate parity (UIRP) condition. $N = 1$, $r^{Sf} = 0.04$, $r^{\$} = 0.06$, and $E(X_1^{Sf/\$}) = 1.57\ Sf/\$$. *The UIRP condition holds if* $X_{U0}^{Sf/\$} = 1.60\ Sf/\$$: $1.57\ Sf/\$ = 1.60\ Sf/\$(1.04/1.06)$.

As should be clear, one manager's view on the intrinsic spot FX rate will be different from another manager's view, and we really do not know whose view is correct. And banks do not have a magic formula for a currency forecast either.

Bank FX Forecasts: 2004 and 2012

In early February 2004, the *Economist* magazine reported that the average of seven American and European banks' forecasts for the FX price of the euro for one year later was 1.32 $/€. At the time, the one-year U.S. dollar LIBOR was 1.43% and the one-year euro LIBOR was 2.20%. Based on these numbers, the time-0 intrinsic spot FX value of the euro, using the UIRP condition, was 1.33 $/€. At the same time, the actual spot FX rate was 1.255 $/€. Based on the banks' forecasts and the financial market conditions, we'd say that the spot euro was undervalued at the time.

In December 2012, a *Wall Street Journal* article reported that two major European banks, UBS and Société Générale, were forecasting a depreciation of the euro to about 1.20 $/€ by the end of 2013, from the spot FX rate of 1.33 $/€ at the time. Another bank, Morgan Stanley, predicted a "hefty slide" in the Australian dollar.

The argument made by economists that spot FX rates should align with the UIRP condition is based on the assumption that the bulk of the informed FX market traders have the same FX forecast and will quickly exploit any speculative profit opportunities that are available. If the Swiss franc has a lower actual spot FX price than the intrinsic spot FX value under the UIRP condition, traders will presumably see this undervaluation and put on a speculative trading program involving the spot purchase of Swiss francs with the expectation of making a profit. In theory, the pressure of this speculative trading should force today's actual spot FX rate to converge to the spot FX rate that would hold according to the UIRP condition.

For example, if the actual spot FX rate, $X_0^{Sf/\$}$, is 1.65 Sf/$ when the UIRP spot FX rate, $X_{U0}^{Sf/\$}$, is 1.60 Sf/$, the Swissie is currently under-valued relative to its intrinsic FX value under the UIRP condition. Confident in the forecasted time-1 spot FX rate of 1.57 Sf/$, a trader could borrow $1,000 today at 6%, promising to repay $1,060. At the same time, the trader would use the $1,000 to buy Sf 1,650 in the spot FX market, and deposit those Sf 1,650 for a year at 4%, to have Sf 1,650 (1.04) = Sf 1,716 a year from now. (Note that this strategy is not a carry trade, because the borrowing is in the higher interest rate currency.) The trader expects to profit because he expects to exchange the Sf 1,716 into U.S. dollars at 1.57 Sf/$ at the end of the year, to have $1,093. Although the trader puts up no capital at time 0, he expects a profit at time 1 of $1,093 − 1,060 = $33, because he's buying Swiss francs at time 0 at an undervalued spot FX rate relative to the UIRP intrinsic spot FX value. In theory, the pressure of this speculative trading forces today's actual spot FX rate to converge to the spot FX rate that would hold according to the UIRP condition, 1.60 Sf/$.

The one-year interest rate in U.S. dollars is 7% and in yen is 2%. The expected spot FX for a year from now is 104 ¥/$.

(a) What should be the spot FX rate now if the UIRP condition holds?

(b) If the actual spot FX rate now is 107 ¥/$, is the yen undervalued or overvalued relative to the UIRP intrinsic spot FX value?

(c) Show how speculative profit can be made if the actual spot FX rate now is 107 ¥/$.

Answers: (a) You want to find $X_{U0}^{¥/\$}$ such that $E(X_1^{¥/\$})$ = 104 ¥/$= $X_{U0}^{¥/\$}[(1 + r^¥)/(1 + r^\$)] = X_{U0}^{¥/\$}(1.02/1.07)$. Thus, $X_{U0}^{¥/\$}$ = 109.10 ¥/$.

(b) Comparing the actual spot FX rate of 107 ¥/$ to the UIRP spot FX rate of 109.10 ¥/$, the yen is currently overvalued. (c) Because the yen is overvalued, you want to sell yen in the spot FX market. So borrow ¥107,000 and spot FX into $1,000. Deposit the $1,000 at 7% to get $1,070 a year from now, which you expect to convert to $1,070 (104 ¥/$) = ¥111,280. (Technically, this strategy is a carry trade, because you are borrowing the lower interest rate currency and depositing the higher interest rate currency.) Since you need to repay the yen loan with ¥107,000(1.02) = ¥109,140, the trader expects a profit of ¥111,280 − 109,140 = ¥2,140. In U.S. dollars at the expected spot FX rate of 104 ¥/$, the trader expects a profit of ¥2,140/(104 ¥/$) = $20.58.

Note that if the UIRP condition holds, the currency with the higher interest rate is expected to depreciate between time 0 and time N. This result can seem counter-intuitive, because we often think that investors will have a demand for the higher interest rate currency. But remember that if the UIRP condition holds, the current actual spot FX rate has already moved to its (short-run) equilibrium. Economists use the term *equilibrium* to describe a condition that holds or else there will be pressure for the variables in the condition to change until it does hold. Once achieved, the equilibrium condition would tend to change only because of a change in one of the variables. The UIRP condition is an equilibrium relationship.

In the UIRP condition, all potential profit opportunities have already been exploited. If the currency with the higher interest rate was not expected to depreciate, and the currency with the lower interest rate not expected to appreciate, this would not be an equilibrium situation, because speculators could profit by shifting money from the lower interest rate currency to the higher interest rate currency. In theory, money movement like this causes the spot FX price of the higher interest rate currency to rise until equilibrium is reached where money would quit shifting. In theory, if the UIRP condition holds, the equilibrium has already been reached where the spot FX price of the high interest rate currency has already been bid up high enough that the expected future depreciation of the currency leaves investors indifferent between interest-bearing securities in the two currencies.

If the UIRP condition holds, speculators would not expect to profit from carry trades because a higher interest rate currency would tend to depreciate. A carry trader could show a profit for many months, but a crash could erase the profits, so that on average, the carry trade strategy is not profitable. So speculators doing carry trades, and many do, must believe either (a) that the actual spot FX rate and the interest rates are not (yet) consistent with the UIRP condition; or (b) that they will be able to somehow unwind before the crash occurs.

Of course, speculators take risk in the trading strategy that is supposed to enforce the UIRP condition and might lose money. There is no guarantee of profit on a given trade because the eventual spot FX rate is uncertain and might result in a loss.

Short-Run and Long-Run Intrinsic Spot FX Rates

The intrinsic FX rate based on the goods market may be viewed as a long-run intrinsic FX rate, whereas the intrinsic FX rate based on the financial market may be viewed as a short-run intrinsic FX rate. In general, economists think that it is more reasonable for a spot FX rate to align with short-run financial market conditions than with longer-run goods market conditions. We now review some basic ideas of an instructive model that features both short-run and long-run intrinsic FX rates.[1]

The initial setting is as follows: (a) The time-N spot FX rate is expected to be equal to the APPP spot FX rate for all future N. (b) The expected inflation rate is 0 in both the United States and the Eurozone. (c) The interest rate is the same for any maturity in both U.S. dollars and euros. (d) The time-0 short-run (UIRP) intrinsic spot FX rate is equal to the time-0 long-run (APPP) intrinsic spot FX rate, and the time-0 actual spot FX rate is equal to both. For example, initially the time-0 actual spot FX rate is 1 \$/€. Since this spot FX rate is the time-0 APPP intrinsic spot FX rate, and since the inflation rate is zero in both economies, the expected spot FX rate is 1 \$/€ for all future N. Working backward, given the expected future spot FX rate of 1 \$/€ for all future N, and given the equal interest rates of the two currencies, the time-0 actual spot FX rate of 1 \$/€ is also equal to the short-run (UIRP) intrinsic FX rate, consistent with financial market conditions.

Next, let us say that at time 0, the U.S. money supply is suddenly and unexpectedly raised by 10%. Unless this increase results in higher U.S. productivity, all else being the same, goods prices in the United States should rise by 10%. That is, if the initial price level in the United States is \$100, the new price level should be \$110. In monetarist economic theory, the goods price increase is instantaneous at time 0. But in reality, goods prices are "sticky," so the 10% rise in goods prices will occur gradually over time.

Meanwhile, individuals use the additional U.S. money supply to buy U.S. financial assets, causing U.S. interest rates to drop. If the money supply increase is something like the U.S. Fed's quantitative easing "QE3" program in September 2012, the policy goal is for the lower interest rates to stimulate productivity, which hopefully will "outrun" the inflation. To focus on basic ideas, we'll ignore the potential productivity gains for now, and assume that the 10% money supply increase only results in a gradual rise in U.S. goods prices by 10%. For simplicity, we assume that it takes two years for U.S. goods prices to undergo the 10% adjustment to the higher money supply, and that the financial market expects this adjustment in this time frame. After two years have passed, and U.S. goods prices have risen by 10%, the new long-run intrinsic spot FX rate, per the goods market and the APPP condition, will be 1.10 \$/€. To see this point, think about a time-0 Eurozone price level of €100, consistent with the \$100 U.S. price level and the time-0 APPP spot FX rate of 1 \$/€; then if the U.S. price level rises by 10%, to \$110, the new APPP spot FX rate is \$110/€100 = 1.10 \$/€. So the new expected time-2 intrinsic spot FX rate is higher due to the expected U.S. inflation.

We also assume that at time 0, the one-year U.S. dollar interest rate suddenly drops from 5% to 4% when the U.S. money supply rises. Then, as U.S. goods prices gradually rise over the next two years, the one-year U.S. dollar interest rate will gradually revert back to 5%. For simplicity, assume that the one-year U.S. dollar interest rate rises by 50 basis points per year, from 4% at time 0 to 4.5% at time 1, and then to 5% at time 2.

Now we find the new time-0 short-run intrinsic FX rate per the UIRP condition. We start with the expected time-2 spot FX rate and work backward, applying the UIRP condition year-by-year.

The expected time-2 spot FX rate is the new expected time-2 APPP intrinsic spot FX rate, 1.10 $/€. Because we project the time-1 one-year euro and U.S. dollar interest rates to be 5% and 4.5%, respectively, we solve equation (5.1) to get a time-1 spot FX rate consistent with the UIRP condition: 1.10 $/€ = $X_{UI}^{\$/€}$(1.045/1.05); so $X_{UI}^{\$/€}$ = 1.105 $/€. We now use this time-1 spot FX rate as the expected time-1 spot FX rate, and work backward again. Because the time-0 one-year euro and U.S. dollar interest rates are 5% and 4%, respectively, we solve equation (5.1) to get a time-0 spot FX rate: 1.105 $/€ = $X_{U0}^{\$/€}$(1.04/1.05); so $X_{U0}^{\$/€}$ = 1.116 $/€. This is the new time-0 short-run intrinsic spot FX rate.

The impact of the time-0 U.S. dollar interest rate drop is thus an immediate rise in the time-0 short-run intrinsic spot FX rate, from 1 $/€ to 1.116 $/€, an immediate appreciation of the euro. Meanwhile, the time-0 long-run intrinsic spot FX rate is still 1 $/€, consistent with the APPP condition at time 0, because goods prices have not yet changed. As we see, the new time-0 short-run intrinsic spot FX rate is not consistent with the time-0 long-run intrinsic spot FX rate. Indeed, the short-run intrinsic spot FX rate will not be equal to the long-run intrinsic spot FX rate for the next two years. But, day-by-day, the short-run intrinsic spot FX rate remains consistent with the UIRP condition and financial market conditions (interest rates).

The new short-run intrinsic spot FX rate, 1.116 $/€, is said to "overshoot" the new expected time-2 long-run intrinsic spot FX rate, 1.10 $/€. Note also that if the time-0 actual spot FX rate jumps to 1.116 $/€, the euro is expected to gradually depreciate from 1.116 $/€ to 1.10 $/€. So an empirical analysis of the RPPP condition during this time period will find contrary evidence: The economy with the lower inflation rate (the Eurozone) will have the currency that depreciates. Figure 5.2 depicts the result of the 10% shock to the U.S. money supply.

In the next example, we assume that the "easing" results in productivity increases that preempt future goods price increases.

A. Initial situation

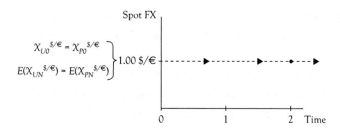

$$X_{U0}^{\$/€} = X_{P0}^{\$/€}$$
$$E(X_{UN}^{\$/€}) = E(X_{PN}^{\$/€})$$

1.00 $/€

Spot FX

0   1   2 Time

B. After money supply shock

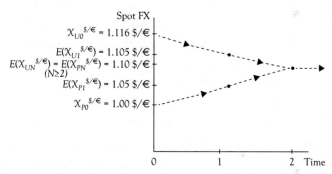

$$X_{U0}^{\$/€} = 1.116\ \$/€$$
$$E(X_{U1}^{\$/€}) = 1.105\ \$/€$$
$$E(X_{UN}^{\$/€}) = E(X_{PN}^{\$/€}) = 1.10\ \$/€$$
$$(N≥2)$$
$$E(X_{P1}^{\$/€}) = 1.05\ \$/€$$
$$X_{P0}^{\$/€} = 1.00\ \$/€$$

Spot FX

0   1   2 Time

Figure 5.2. Effect of Upward Shock in U.S. Money Supply (10%).

Initial assumptions: The actual time-0 spot FX rate is 1.40 $/€ and is equal to both the long-run and short-run intrinsic spot FX rates; the interest rate is 4% for any maturity in both U.S. dollars and euros; the expected inflation rate is 0 in both the United States and the Eurozone.

Assume next: The U.S. Fed raises the U.S. money supply by 15% with the following results:

(a) At time 0, the one-year U.S. dollar interest rate instantaneously drops from 4% to 2.5%.

(b) The lower U.S. dollar interest rate stimulates U.S. productivity, which outruns and preempts any future U.S. goods price increases. So the United States experiences no inflation after the easing.

(c) Over the next three years, the one-year U.S. dollar interest rate will gradually revert back to 4%. For simplicity, assume that the-one-year U.S. dollar interest rate will rise by 50 basis points per year, to 3% at time 1, to 3.5% at time 2, and finally to 4% at time 3.

(A) Find the new expected time-3 APPP intrinsic spot FX rate.

(B) Find the new time-0 short-run intrinsic spot FX rate consistent with financial market conditions.

Answers: (A) Because U.S. goods prices are not expected to change after the money supply increase, the new expected time-3 APPP intrinsic spot FX rate is unchanged, 1.40 $/€. (B) The time-3 forecasted spot FX rate is the time-3 APPP intrinsic FX rate, 1.40 $/€. Because we project that at time 2, the one-year euro and U.S. dollar interest rates will be 4% and 3.5%, respectively, we solve equation (5.1) to get a time-2 projected intrinsic spot FX rate of 1.407 $/€, which we now use as the expected time-2 spot FX rate. Working backward, because we project that the time-1 one-year euro and U.S. dollar interest rates will be 4% and 3%, respectively, we solve equation (5.1) again, to get a time-1 projected intrinsic spot FX rate of 1.42 $/€, which becomes the expected time-1 spot FX rate. Because the time-0 one-year euro and U.S. dollar interest rates are 4% and 2.5%, respectively, we solve equation (5.1) again, for the time-0 short-run intrinsic spot FX rate of 1.44 $/€.

Empirical Evidence on Uncovered Interest Rate Parity

Finance researchers have conducted numerous empirical tests of the UIRP theory with historical data. The studies typically check whether a currency with a higher interest rate has tended to depreciate relative to a currency with a lower interest rate. The results of these empirical studies, however, are often the *opposite* of what the UIRP theory would predict. That is, on average, currencies with lower interest rates have tended to subsequently depreciate, and currencies with higher interest rates have tended to appreciate, exactly the opposite of the prediction of the UIRP condition. These empirical findings are known as the *forward premium puzzle* (for a reason we explain later.)

Summary of Empirical Research on the UIRP Condition

	UIRP condition	Empirical evidence
Higher interest rate currency	↓	↑
Lower interest rate currency	↑	↓

The arrows show the direction of change in spot FX rates. The UIRP condition implies that the higher interest rate currency should tend to depreciate and the currency lower interest rate currency should tend to appreciate. The historical data show that the opposite tends to happen.

The empirical trends revealed in the UIRP condition tests mainly occur for currencies of developed countries and mainly when the U.S. dollar has the higher interest rate. The UIRP prediction, of a gradual depreciation of the currency with the higher interest rate, is more reliable when an emerging market country is involved. This finding is reasonable, because higher interest rates are more likely to reflect higher inflation rates in emerging market countries.[2]

Consider two possible reasons for why the historical data do not support the UIRP condition. One possibility is the market functions well, but that market participants tend to systematically underestimate the expected future spot FX value of the higher interest rate currency. In this environment, the UIRP condition "holds," but with the market's incorrect forecast of the spot FX rate rather than the true expected spot FX rate. To see this point with an example, assume $N = 1$, $r^{Sf} = 0.04$, and $r^{\$} = 0.06$. Say the true expected spot FX rate is $E(X_I^{Sf/\$}) = 1.57$ Sf/\$, but traders incorrectly forecast the future FX rate is 1.50 Sf/\$. The theory behind the UIRP condition says that today's spot FX rate would be $X_{U0}^{Sf/\$} = 1.53$ Sf/\$, solving equation (5.1) using 1.50 Sf/\$ as the expected future spot FX rate. Say that the UIRP condition holds in that today's actual spot FX rate is also 1.53 Sf/\$. Given that the true expected FX rate is 1.57 Sf/\$, however, empirical tests by researchers will find that the higher interest rate currency, the U.S. dollar, tends to appreciate rather than depreciate. In this case, the empirical evidence conflicts with the UIRP theory, but actually the UIRP condition holds; traders are just bad forecasters of the future FX rate.

The one-year interest rate in U.S. dollars is 3% and in euros is 6%. The consensus expected spot FX for a year from now is 1.40 $/€. The true (but unknown) expected spot FX for a year from now is 1.50 $/€. Assume the UIRP condition holds with the consensus forecast.

(a) What is today's spot FX rate?

(b) Which currency do traders expect to depreciate, given that the UIRP condition holds with their forecast?

(c) Is the true (unobservable) expected change in the spot FX rate consistent or inconsistent with the empirical findings about the UIRP theory?

Answers: (a) The UIRP intrinsic spot FX value of the euro is 1.44 $/€, because 1.40 $/€ = 1.44 $/€(1.03/1.06). (b) The traders forecast the euro to depreciate from 1.44 $/€ today to 1.40 $/€ a year from now, because the interest rate for the euro is higher. (c) The true expectation is that the euro will appreciate, despite having the higher interest rate, which is consistent with the empirical evidence.

The second interpretation of the empirical evidence is that FX market participants make adequate FX forecasts, but the market does not function efficiently. That is, FX trading activity is insufficient to instantaneously enforce the actual time-0 spot FX rate into equality with the short-run intrinsic spot FX rate. Perhaps in reality it takes longer for markets to equilibrate than the instantaneous horizon of the theory. For example, assume again that $N = 1$, $r^{Sf} = 0.04$, and $r^{\$} = 0.06$, and that traders' forecast of the time-1 spot FX rate is equal to the true expected spot FX rate, 1.50 Sf/$. Say that the time-0 spot FX rate is initially the same as the short-run financial market intrinsic FX rate, $X_0^{Sf/\$} = X_{U0}^{Sf/\$} = 1.53$ Sf/$. Now assume that the one-year U.S. dollar interest rate suddenly jumps at time 0 by 50 basis points, to 0.065. Given no change in traders' FX forecast, the time-0 spot FX rate should instantaneously change to 1.536 Sf/$ in order to reestablish equilibrium. But if in reality the FX market reacts gradually rather than instantaneously, then there will be a period of time where the U.S. dollar gradually rises from 1.53 Sf/$ to 1.536 Sf/$. During this time period, the evidence will appear to refute the UIRP condition, because the currency with the higher interest rate, the U.S. dollar, appreciates.

The most common way you will see the UIRP condition presented is with the actual time-0 spot FX rate, $X_0^{Sf/\$}$, in equation (5.1) instead of the short-run intrinsic spot FX rate, $X_{U0}^{Sf/\$}$. Of course, the actual time-0 spot FX rate is observable. With this approach, there is a temptation to apply the UIRP condition as a forecasting model. For example, assume $N = 1$, $r^{Sf} = 0.04$, $r^{\$} = 0.06$, and the actual spot FX rate, $X_0^{Sf/\$}$, is 1.65 Sf/$. If we plug 1.65 Sf/$ for $X_{U0}^{Sf/\$}$ in equation (5.1), we may solve for the unknown, $E(X_1^{Sf/\$}) = 1.65$ Sf/$(1.04/1.06) = 1.62 Sf/$. Note that if we want to apply the UIRP condition in this popular way as a forecasting model, we must be willing to buy into the assumption that the UIRP condition holds, and we have seen that the empirical evidence is not very encouraging on this approach.

The one-year interest rate in U.S. dollars is 3% and in euros is 6%. Today's actual spot FX is 1.40 $/€. Assume the UIRP condition holds. What is the expected spot FX rate for a year from now?

Answer: 1.40 $/€(1.03/1.06) = 1.36 $/€.

Despite the apparent lack of fit with actual data in research studies, the UIRP condition is a very useful model. The theory is based on instructive reasoning, and we have seen how the model helps us understand some of the forces that should and do drive FX prices. Moreover, the UIRP model helps us tell when a currency is overvalued or undervalued.

Summary Action Points

- Carry trades, involving borrowing in low interest rate currencies and investing in high interest rate currencies, have a significant impact on FX markets.
- The UIRP condition is an economic theory that actual spot FX rates should align with interest rates and predictions of future FX spot rates.

- In the UIRP condition, the currency with the higher (lower) interest rate is expected to depreciate (appreciate).
- The intrinsic spot FX rate in the UIRP theory is a short-run intrinsic FX rate. A short-run intrinsic FX rate does not have to be equal to the long-run intrinsic FX rate, based on goods prices, and the actual spot FX rate may not be equal to either intrinsic spot FX rate.
- The economic activity needed to enforce the UIRP condition is not easy, so it should not be surprising that actual FX rates would deviate from the UIRP standard of intrinsic FX value. Although this issue is difficult to test and interpret, researchers believe that actual historical FX rate and interest rate data do not fit the implications of the UIRP theory.
- Models of intrinsic FX value are useful even if they don't "fit" the data, because we get an idea of whether a currency is misvalued and may be due for a correction.

Glossary

Carry trade: See Currency carry trade.

Currency carry trade: Borrowing in a lower interest rate currency and investing the exchanged proceeds in a higher interest rate currency deposit. This is a common speculative trade based on the belief that the high interest rate currency will not depreciate by as much as would be the case if the UIRP condition holds.

Dornbusch model: An economic theory of intrinsic spot FX rates where the short-run (financial market) intrinsic spot FX rate differs from the long-run (goods market) intrinsic spot FX rate.

Eurocurrency: A time deposit or time loan in a currency, traded globally at market interest rates.

Eurodollar: A time deposit or time loan in U.S. dollars, traded globally at market interest rates.

Equilibrium: A condition that holds or else there will be pressure for the variables in the condition to change until it does hold. One achieved, the equilibrium condition would tend to change only because of a change in one of the variables.

Equilibrium FX rate: A term used by economists that is a synonym for intrinsic FX rate.

Fisher open equation: The UIRP condition.

International Fisher equation: The UIRP condition.

London interbank offer rate (LIBOR): An index of the interest rate for deposits and loans of a given currency and a given maturity.

Short-run intrinsic FX rate: The spot FX rate that represents the spot FX rate consistent with financial market conditions, namely, interest rates.

Uncovered interest rate parity condition (UIRP): The theoretical economic relationship between the spot FX rate, the expected future spot FX rate, and the interest rate differential. Also known as the *International Fisher equation* or the *Fisher open equation*.

Discussion Questions

1. Explain the difference between a short-run intrinsic FX rate and a long-run intrinsic FX rate.

2. Explain what a carry trade is and how carry trades have affected FX rates.

3. Discuss the following statement: The UIRP condition is useful because the implications of the model are not consistent with empirical data.

4. Assume that both the APPP and UIRP conditions hold. Explain why a short-run increase in the interest rate for a currency, other things equal, can cause the currency to be overvalued from the perspective of the goods market. Use this reasoning to explain why a country with high economic growth may experience a trade deficit.

Problems

1. The spot FX rate is 1.35 $/€ today. At time 0 (now), the one-year interest rate for euros is 5%, and for U.S. dollars is 3%. The expected spot FX rate a year from now is 1.22 $/€. (A) Using the expected spot FX rate, what is today's intrinsic spot FX rate assuming the UIRP condition holds? (B) Choose (a), (b), or (c): Based on the UIRP condition, (a) the U.S. dollar is undervalued against the euro; (b) the U.S. dollar overvalued against the euro; (c) the currencies are correctly valued or one cannot tell if the currencies are misvalued.

2. The actual spot FX rate is 1 Sf/$ today. At time 0 (now), the one-year interest rate for Swiss francs is 1%, and for U.S. dollars is 3%. The expected spot FX rate a year from now is 1.10 Sf/$. (A) Using the expected spot FX rate, what is today's intrinsic spot FX rate assuming the UIRP condition holds? (B) Choose (a), (b), (c), or (d): Based on the UIRP condition, at time 0: (a) the U.S. dollar is undervalued against the Swiss franc; (b) the U.S. dollar is overvalued against the Swiss franc; (c) the currencies are correctly valued; (d) cannot tell.

3. The one-year interest rate in U.S. dollars is 4% and in British pounds is 6%. Informed traders expect the spot FX rate to be 1.84 $/£ a year from now. (a) What is the current spot FX rate if the UIRP condition holds? (b) If the actual spot FX rate at time 0 is 1.85 $/£, is the pound undervalued or overvalued relative to the UIRP standard of intrinsic FX value? (c) How can a trader create an expected profit situation if the actual time-0 spot FX rate is 1.85 $/£?

4. Assume that the actual current spot FX rate of 1.35 $/€ is initially consistent with both the long-run (APPP) intrinsic spot FX rate and the short-run (UIRP) intrinsic spot FX rate. Assume that initially the annualized interest rate is 4% for any maturity in both U.S. dollars and euros, and the expected inflation rate is 0 in both the United States and the Eurozone. Assume the U.S. money supply is suddenly increased by 15% and that it takes one year for U.S. goods prices to gradually rise by 15%. Assume that at time 0, the one-year U.S. dollar interest rate suddenly drops from 4% to 3% when the U.S. money supply rises. (a) Find the new expected time-1 APPP spot FX rate. (b) Find the new time-0 short-run intrinsic spot FX rate consistent with financial market conditions.

5. Assume that the actual current spot FX rate of 1.25 $/€ is initially consistent with both the long-run (APPP) intrinsic spot FX rate and the short-run (UIRP) intrinsic spot FX rate. Assume that initially the annualized interest rate is 6% for any maturity in both U.S. dollars and euros, and the expected inflation rate is 0 in both the United States and the Eurozone. Assume the U.S. money supply is suddenly increased by 10%. Assume that it takes three years for U.S. goods prices to rise by 10%. Assume that at time 0, the one-year U.S. dollar interest rate suddenly drops from 6% to 4.5% when the U.S. money

supply rises. Assume that the one-year U.S. dollar interest rate rises to 5% at time 1, to 5.5% at time 2, and finally to 6% at time 3. (a) Find the new expected time-3 APPP intrinsic spot FX rate. (b) Find the new time-0 short-run intrinsic spot FX rate consistent with financial market conditions.

6. The one-year interest rate in U.S. dollars is 6% and in euros is 3%. The consensus expected spot FX for a year from now is 1.50 $/€. The true (but unknown) expected spot FX for a year from now is 1.40 $/€. Assume the UIRP condition holds with the consensus forecast. (a) What is the UIRP intrinsic spot FX rate? (b) Which currency do traders expect to appreciate? (c) Is the true (unknown) expected change in the spot FX rate consistent or inconsistent with the empirical findings about the UIRP theory?

7. The one-year interest rate in U.S. dollars is 6% and in euros is 3%. Today's actual spot FX is 1.40 $/€. Assume the UIRP condition holds. What is the expected spot FX rate for a year from now?

Answers to Problems

1. (A) The theoretical spot FX rate, given financial market conditions and the market FX forecast, is $X_{U0}^{\$/€}$ in 1.22 $/€ = $X_{U0}^{\$/€}(1.03/1.05)$, so $X_{U0}^{\$/€} = 1.24$ $/€.

   (B) (a) The euro is overvalued, and the U.S. dollar is undervalued.

2. (A) 1.10 Sf/$ = $X_{U0}^{Sf/\$}(1.01/1.03)$; so $X_{U0}^{Sf/\$} = 1.12$ Sf/$.

   (B) (a) The U.S. dollar is undervalued against the Swiss franc.

3. (a) You want to find $X_{U0}^{\$/£}$ such that $X_{U0}^{\$/£}[(1 + r^\$)/(1 + r^£)] = E(X_1^{\$/£}) = 1.84$ $/£ $= X_{U0}^{\$/£}(1.04/1.06)$. Thus, $X_{U0}^{\$/£} = 1.875$ $/£.

   (b) At an actual spot FX rate of 1.85 $/£, the British pound is undervalued relative to the UIRP intrinsic spot FX rate.

   (c) Because the British pound is undervalued, a trader wants to buy pounds in the spot FX market. To do this, borrow $1,850, and spot FX into £1,000; deposit the £1,000 at 6% for a year to get £1,060, which the trader expects to FX back into £1,060(1.84 $/£) = $1,950.40. Because the trader owes $1,850(1.04) = $1,924 on the U.S. dollar loan, the expected profit is $1,950.40 − 1,924 = $26.40.

4. (a) New expected time-1 APPP spot FX rate is 1.35 $/€(1.15) = 1.55 $/€.

   (b) New time-0 spot FX rate consistent with the short-run (financial market) intrinsic spot FX rate: 1.55 $/€ = (New $X_{U0}^{\$/€}$)(1.03/1.04); New $X_{U0}^{\$/€}$ = 1.57 $/€.

5. (a) Because U.S. goods price should rise by 10% after the money supply increase of 10%, the new expected time-3 APPP spot FX rate is 1.10(1.25 $/€) = 1.375 $/€.

   (b) The time-3 forecasted spot FX rate is the new expected time-3 APPP spot FX rate, 1.375 $/€. Because at time 2, the one-year euro interest rate is projected to be 6% and the one-year U.S. dollar interest rate is projected to be 5.5%, we solve equation (5.1) to get a time-2 intrinsic spot FX rate of 1.3815 $/€, which we now use as the expected time-2 spot FX rate. Since at time 1, the one-year euro interest rate is projected to be 6% and the one-year U.S. dollar interest rate is projected to be 5%, we solve equation (5.1) to get a time-1 intrinsic spot FX rate of 1.395 $/€, which we now use as the expected time-1 spot FX rate. Because at time 0, the one-year euro interest rate is projected to be 6% and the one-year U.S. dollar interest rate is 4.5%, we solve equation (5.1) to get a new time-0 short-run intrinsic spot FX rate of 1.415 $/€.

6. (a) The UIRP intrinsic spot FX rate is 1.46 $/€, because 1.50 $/€ = 1.46 $/€(1.06/1.03).

   (b) The euro is expected to appreciate from 1.46 $/€ today to 1.50 $/€ a year from now, because the interest rate for the euro is lower.

   (c) The true (unknown) expectation is that the euro will *depreciate*, from 1.46 $/€ today to 1.40 $/€ a year from now, despite having the lower interest rate, which is consistent with the empirical findings.

7. 1.40 $/€(1.06/1.03) = 1.44 $/€.

CHAPTER 6

Topics in Uncovered Interest Rate Parity

This chapter covers some applications and issues related to the uncovered interest rate parity (UIRP) condition. We first show the simple expected rate of change of the short-run intrinsic foreign exchange (FX) rate, given the UIRP condition. This concept has important implications in international finance, including converting an asset's cost of capital from one currency into another.

The chapter also analyzes the impact on the spot FX rate if a currency's interest rate abruptly changes. This exercise is intended to help us see the dynamic forces that affect FX rates.

We shall also describe Siegel's paradox, which is a minor mathematical problem for the UIRP theory. Finally, we shall cover the idea of how real interest rates connect the short-run intrinsic FX rate (consistent with financial market conditions and the UIRP condition) with the long-run intrinsic FX rate (consistent with goods market conditions and the absolute purchasing power parity (APPP) condition.)

Expected Rate of Short-Run Intrinsic FX Change

If the spot FX rate is correctly valued relative to financial market conditions, the expected rate of FX change is the *expected rate of short-run intrinsic FX change*. The notation $E^*(x^{Sf/\$})$ denotes the expected annualized percentage change in the short-run intrinsic spot FX price of the U.S. dollar (relative to the Swiss franc), where the asterisk conveys the notion of short-run intrinsic FX valuation consistent with financial market conditions. If the UIRP condition is the correct model of short-run intrinsic FX value in the financial market, the expected rate of short-run intrinsic FX change is given as a linear approximation in equation (6.1):

Expected Rate of Short-Run Intrinsic FX Change
Linear Approximation UIRP Condition

$$E^*(x^{Sf/\$}) = r^{Sf} - r^{\$} \qquad (6.1)$$

In equation (6.1), the interest rate for the "denominator currency" is subtracted from the interest rate of the "numerator currency." Let us do a numerical example. Assume $r^{Sf} = 0.04$, and $r^{\$} = 0.06$. The linear approximation in equation (6.1) says that $E^*(x^{Sf/\$}) = 0.04 - 0.06 = -0.02$, or −2%. By way of comparison with the UIRP condition in equation (5.1), assume $E(X_1^{Sf/\$}) = 1.57$ Sf/\$. Thus the UIRP condition in equation (5.1) says that today's spot FX rate should be $X_{U0}^{Sf/\$} = 1.60$ Sf/\$. The expected rate of intrinsic spot FX change, given that the UIRP condition holds, is (1.57 Sf/\$)/(1.60 Sf/\$) − 1 = −0.019, or −1.9%, so the linear approximation in equation (6.1) is close.[1]

Assume the one-year interest rates for the U.S. dollar and the euro are 5.8% and 3.5%, respectively. Find the approximate one-year expected rate of short-run intrinsic FX change of the euro using equation (6.1).

Answer: $E^*(x^{\$/€}) = r^{\$} - r^{€} = 0.058 - 0.035 = 0.023$ or 2.3%.

If the UIRP condition does not hold, the expected rate of actual FX change will differ from the expected rate of intrinsic FX change. For example, assume: (a) the expected time-1 spot FX rate is 1.57 Sf/\$; (b) the time-0 spot FX rate that should hold if the UIRP condition holds is 1.60 Sf/\$; and (c) the time-0 actual spot FX rate is 1.50 Sf/\$. Then the expected rate of actual FX change over the next year is (1.57 Sf/\$)/(1.50 Sf/\$) − 1 = 0.0467, or 4.67%, whereas the expected rate of intrinsic FX change is −1.9%, as we found above.

Note that we can find the expected rate of short-run intrinsic FX change using the UIRP condition, or the approximation version in equation (6.1), even if the UIRP condition does not hold in reality. The expected rate of short-run intrinsic FX change has uses in international finance, including converting an asset's cost of capital from one currency to another, regardless of whether the actual FX rate is equal to the intrinsic FX rate of the UIRP condition.

Asset Market Approach to Interest Rate Shocks

There are two polar extremes of economic theory on how interest rate shocks affect FX rates. They are referred to as the *asset market approach* and the *Fisher approach*. The asset market approach assumes short-run intrinsic FX rates consistent with financial market conditions and the UIRP condition. The Fisher approach assumes that FX rates are always equal to long-run (APPP) intrinsic FX rates, and that interest rate changes are always driven by changes in expected inflation.

We first look more closely at the asset market approach. We start with the assumptions that the one-year $r^{Sf} = 4\%$, the one-year $r^{\$} = 6\%$, and the expected time-1 spot FX rate is $E(X_1^{Sf/\$}) = 1.57$ Sf/$. We assume the UIRP condition holds, so that the current spot FX rate $X_0^{Sf/\$} = 1.60$ Sf/$. Using equation (6.1), the U.S. dollar is expected to depreciate by approximately 2%. Using equation (5.1), the U.S. dollar is expected to depreciate by 1.875%, because $(1.57 \text{ Sf/}\$)/(1.60 \text{ Sf/}\$) - 1 = -0.01875$. Suppose that the one-year Swiss franc interest rate unexpectedly rises overnight from 4% to 4.50%. What should happen to the spot FX rate?

In the asset market approach, the unexpected rise in the Swiss franc interest rate is not due to a change in inflation expectations, but is instead due to something like an unexpected hike in the discount rate by Switzerland's central bank, the Swiss National Bank. In this case, the interest rate shock results in an immediate appreciation of the Swiss franc. The reason is that financial capital will flow into Swiss francs to capture the higher return, causing the Swiss franc to rise. Given that $E(X_1^{Sf/\$})$ stays at 1.57 Sf/$, the new time-0 spot FX rate that will re-establish the UIRP condition, given the new Swiss franc interest rate of 4.50%, can be found using equation (5.1), $1.57 \text{ Sf/}\$ = X_0^{Sf/\$}(1.045/1.06)$, implying the *new* $X_0^{Sf/\$}$ = 1.592 Sf/$. We see that the time-0 spot FX price of the Swiss franc rises, because the time-0 spot FX rate changes from 1.60 Sf/$ to 1.592 Sf/$.

In theory, the spot FX change is presumed to take place "instantaneously" at time 0. Because the expected time-1 spot FX is unchanged, the U.S. dollar is still predicted to depreciate gradually to 1.57 Sf/$. Given the new time-0 spot FX rate of 1.592 Sf/$, the expected depreciation of the U.S. dollar is at a slower rate between time 0 and time 1, reflecting the lower difference between the U.S. dollar and Swiss franc interest rates. By equation (6.1), the new expected rate of FX change in the U.S. dollar is approximately 4.5% – 6% = –1.5%. By equation (5.1), the new expected rate of FX change in the U.S. dollar is exactly (1.57 Sf/$)/ (1.592 Sf/$) – 1 = –0.0138, or –1.38%.

A hike in the discount rate by a central bank is designed to help raise the current spot FX price of the currency, and vice versa. A higher interest rate is intended to attract foreign investors, and the consequent movement of funds to buy the currency causes the current spot FX price to increase. Of course, the dynamics work in reverse if the interest rate drops, all else being the same. Actually, the Swiss National Bank did *lower* the discount rate in August 2011, for the express purpose of trying to cause the spot FX price of the Swiss franc to drop. The reason was that the central bank thought the Swiss franc was overvalued.

Fisher Approach to Interest Rate Shocks

Now let us look at the Fisher approach. An implicit assumption in the Fisher approach is the equality of real rates of interest among countries. Given this assumption, when an interest rate changes, the only reason is that inflation expectations have changed, and the change in the interest rate is necessary to ensure that the real rate of interest does not change. Because the interest rate change reflects a change in the expected inflation rate, there is a change in the expected time-1 APPP FX rate. But the time-0 APPP spot FX rate does not change because the time-0 goods prices do not change. Thus, in the Fisher approach, there is *no* immediate reaction in the time-0 spot FX rate. Instead, the change in the expected inflation rate dictates a different expected time-1 spot FX rate. You can see this by recalling the relative purchasing power parity (RPPP) condition. The Fisher approach, where inflation rate changes drive any and all interest rate changes, is thus based on a long-run, goods market approach to FX value.

For example, assume again that the one-year r^{Sf} = 4%, the one-year $r^{\$}$ = 6%, and the expected time-1 spot FX rate is $E(X_1^{Sf/\$})$ = 1.57 Sf/$. Assume again that the UIRP condition holds, so that the initial current spot FX rate $X_0^{Sf/\$}$ = 1.60 Sf/$. Now assume again that the Swiss franc interest rate suddenly increases from r^{Sf} = 4% to 4.50%. This time, however, the cause of the jump is new information about an increase in the anticipated Swiss franc inflation rate. The jump in the Swiss franc interest rate ensures that the real rate of interest stays the same although higher inflation is anticipated.

Given that the anticipated Swiss inflation rate suddenly increases, the expected time-1 spot FX rate is revised from the initial expectation of 1.57 Sf/$. There is no impact on the time-0 spot FX rate, which stays at 1.60 Sf/$. From the UIRP condition, the new expected time-1 spot FX rate is 1.60 Sf/$(1.045/1.06) = 1.58 Sf/$. This new forecast represents a drop in the expected time-1 spot FX price of the Swiss franc, because of the hike in the expected Swiss inflation rate.

Because the time-0 spot FX is unchanged, the U.S. dollar is still predicted to depreciate gradually over the next year. At the new expected time-1 spot FX rate of 1.58 Sf/$, the expected depreciation of the U.S. dollar is at a slower rate between time 0 and time 1, reflecting the lower difference between the U.S. dollar and Swiss franc interest rates. By equation (6.1), the new expected rate of FX change in the U.S. dollar is approximately 4.5% − 6% = −1.5%. By equation (5.1), the new expected rate of FX change in the U.S. dollar is exactly (1.58 Sf/$)/(1.60 Sf/$) − 1 = −0.0125, or −1.25%.

In summary, an interest rate shock affects *the current spot FX rate* in *the asset market approach*; the expected future spot FX rate is not affected. An interest rate shock affects the *expected future spot FX rate* in *the Fisher approach*; the current spot FX rate is not affected.

Asset market approach	Current spot FX rate affected
	Interest rate shock NOT driven by inflation shock
Fisher approach	Expected future FX rate affected
	Interest rate shock IS driven by inflation shock

The next example covers these ideas using FX rates in American terms. The diagram in Figure 6.1 is based on the numbers in the next example.

Assume the time-0 spot FX rate is 1.60 $/£. And the initial one-year U.S. dollar and pound sterling interest rates are 5% and 10%, respectively. Now let the one-year sterling interest rate jump unexpectedly to 12% at time 0.

(a) Use the UIRP condition to determine what spot FX rate change occurs, if any, assuming the asset market approach.

(b) If the change in the sterling interest rate is due to revised inflation expectations (Fisher approach), find the impact on the current spot FX rate, if any.

(c) Find the expected rate of FX change in the British pound, before and after the interest rate change, for both the asset market and Fisher approaches.

Answers: (a) The initially expected time-1 spot FX rate is (1.60 $/£) (1.05/1.10) = 1.527 $/£. If the sterling interest rate jumps to 12%, the new time-0 spot FX rate is (1.527 $/£)/(1.05/1.12) = 1.63 $/£. (b) The current spot FX rate does not change, but the expected future spot FX rate changes to (1.60 $/£)(1.05/1.12) = 1.50 $/£. (c) Initially, the British pound is expected to depreciate by approximately 5%, because 5% – 10% = –5%, or by exactly 4.56%, because (1.527 $/£)/(1.60 $/£) – 1 = –0.0456, or –4.56%. After the interest rate increases, the pound is expected to depreciate by approximately 7%, because 5% – 12% = –7%. For the asset market approach, the pound is expected to depreciate by exactly 6.32%, because (1.527 $/£)/(1.63 $/£) – 1 = –0.0632, or –6.32%. For the Fisher approach, the pound is expected to depreciate by exactly 6.25%, because (1.50 $/£)/(1.60 $/£) – 1 = –0.0625, or –6.25%.

Asset Market Approach, Fisher Approach, and Reality

The Fisher model of international finance dates to a time when the international financial markets were less developed and goods trade had the dominant impact on FX rates. Fisher's argument that the real rate of interest is the same across all economies in the world is a *very* long-run

A. Initial situation

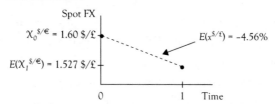

B. Asset market approach

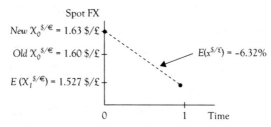

C. Fisher approach

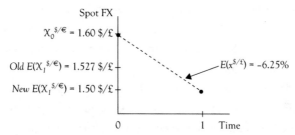

Figure 6.1. Impact of upward shock to British pound interest rate.

equilibrium point of view. The argument is that if the real rates of interest in two economies are not equal, forces should work to drive the two rates into equilibrium. But the reality is that real rates of interest differ between economies for very long periods of time.

The asset market approach is the more modern model, consistent with the international integration of financial markets. For this reason, the asset market approach has more appeal. But the situation is not one of deciding which of the two approaches is better. Both approaches have insights, and so we covered both. Reality is somewhere in between the two polar extremes, or possibly beyond the scope of either approach.

For example, it certainly seems plausible that an interest rate change can simultaneously affect *both* the spot FX rate and the expected spot FX rate, perhaps by affecting other economic variables that are not explicit in the UIRP condition. In some cases, an interest rate increase can slow an economy (perhaps by design of the monetary authorities). If so, investors may revise their expected future FX price of the currency downward without thinking in terms of inflation. The result could in turn lead to a decline in the current spot FX price of the currency.

Canada had this kind of effect in the early 1990s. The Bank of Canada raised short-term interest rates, intending to prop up the Canadian dollar, but the FX market perceived the hike as negative for the Canadian economy, so the spot FX price of the Canadian dollar actually fell in response. In 2000, the euro similarly fell when the European Central Bank (ECB) announced it would raise short-term interest rates. The market expected the move to hinder economic growth.

In the United States, a rise in interest rates in 1994 was coupled with a depreciation of the U.S. dollar relative to other major currencies. The reason turned out to be that, as interest rates rose and bond prices fell, foreign investors in long-term U.S. bonds decided to get out of the U.S. bond market. Their sale of U.S. dollars into other currencies caused the spot FX price of the U.S. dollar to drop. Then the consequent depreciation of the U.S. dollar was further reason for squeamish foreign investors to pull out.

In summary, the actual impact of a change in an interest rate depends on (a) the cause of the interest rate change, and (b) the anticipated collateral impact of the change on other economic variables that relate to FX rates.

Siegel's Paradox

A technical issue with the UIRP condition is known as *Siegel's paradox*. Although $X_N^{\$/€}$ will always be equal to $1/X_N^{€/\$}$, the expected future spot FX rate, $E(X_N^{\$/€})$, cannot be equal to $1/E(X_N^{€/\$})$. That is, if 1.20 $/€ is the expected spot FX price of the euro a year from now, the expected spot FX price of the U.S. dollar *cannot be* $1/(1.20\ \$/€) = 0.833\ €/\$$, although it is true that if the actual spot FX price of the euro will be 1.20 $/€ a year from now, then the actual spot FX price of the U.S. dollar a year from now will exactly be $1/(1.20\ \$/€) = 0.833\ €/\$$.

To see this point, assume there are two equally likely possible outcomes for the future spot FX rate for a year from now: 0.80 $/€ ($\equiv$ 1.25 €/$) and 1.60 $/€ ($\equiv$ 0.625 €/$).

Probability	0.50	0.50
$X_1^{\$/\text{€}}$	0.80 $/€	1.60 $/€
$X_1^{\text{€}/\$}$	1.25 €/$	0.625 €/$

The expected spot FX price of the euro for a year from now is thus 0.50(0.80 $/€) + 0.50(1.60 $/€) = 1.20 $/€. At the same time, the expected spot FX price of the U.S. dollar for a year from now is 0.50 (1.25 €/$) + 0.50(0.625 €/$) = 0.9375 €/$. You see that $1/E(X_1^{\$/\text{€}})$ = 1/(1.20 $/€) = 0.833 €/$ is not equal to $E(X_1^{\text{€}/\$})$, which we computed directly, 0.9375 €/$. Basically, we have shown the mathematical condition that "the mean of a reciprocal is not equal to the reciprocal of a mean."[2]

Assume that the time-0 spot FX rate is 0.90 $/€. A year from now, there is a 50% chance that the spot FX rate will be 0.75 $/€ and a 50% chance that the spot FX rate will be 1.10 $/€.

(a) What is the expected time-1 spot FX rate?

(b) Find the expected time-1 spot FX price of the U.S. dollar. Show Siegel's paradox, that the second answer is not the reciprocal of the first.

Answers: (a) $E(X_1^{\$/\text{€}})$ = 0.50(0.75 $/€) + 0.50(1.10 $/€) = 0.925 $/€;
(b) $E(X_1^{\text{€}/\$})$ = 0.50[1/(0.75 $/€)] + 0.50[1/(1.10 $/€)] = 1.121 €/$;
1/(1.121 €/$) = 0.892 $/€, not 0.925 $/€.

Suppose that the UIRP condition in equation (5.1) holds for the FX rates from the perspective of Sf/$. Since we know that $E(X_N^{\$/Sf})$ ≠ 1/ $E(X_N^{Sf/\$})$, the UIRP condition in equation (5.1) *cannot* hold from the perspective of $/Sf. Because the choice of currency perspective is arbitrary, Siegel's paradox is a minor mathematical problem for UIRP theory. Similarly, note that with the linear approximation in equation (6.1), the UIRP condition says that the expected rate of intrinsic FX change of the euro is equal to the negative expected rate of intrinsic FX change of the U.S. dollar (relative to the euro). That is, $E^*(x^{\text{€}/\$})$ = $-E^*(x^{\$/\text{€}})$. This result also suffers from Siegel's paradox. Despite Siegel's paradox, the UIRP condition and the linear approximation in equation (6.1) are still considered to be useful, because the impact of Siegel's paradox is not major.

International finance theorists have developed a formula to improve the analysis of expected spot FX rates and expected rates of FX change, given Siegel's paradox. The formula is the approximation shown in equation (6.2).[3]

Siegel's Paradox Resolution

Approximation

$$E(x^{\epsilon/\$}) \approx -E(x^{\$/\epsilon}) + \sigma_\epsilon^2 \qquad (6.2)$$

In equation (6.2), σ_ϵ denotes the annualized volatility (standard deviation) of $x^{\$/\epsilon}$. For example, if the euro is expected to appreciate by 2% relative to the U.S. dollar and the annualized volatility of the euro is 0.10, equation (6.2) says that the expected rate of change of the U.S. dollar, relative to the euro, is approximately equal to $-0.02 + 0.10^2 = -0.01$, or -1%. Assume the time-0 spot FX rate is 1.25 $/€, which is equivalent to

Exhibit 6.1. Currency Volatility Estimates

	2002–2007	2007–2012
Australian dollar	0.09	0.13
Brazilian real	0.10	0.14
Euro	0.07	0.10
Indian rupee	0.04	0.08
Japanese yen	0.07	0.09
Mexican peso	0.06	0.11
New Zealand dollar	0.09	0.13
South African rand	0.12	0.14
South Korean won	0.05	0.11
Swedish krona	0.09	0.11
Swiss franc	0.08	0.11
Taiwan dollar	0.04	0.05
UK pound	0.07	0.09

Source: Author's computations using month-end data from St. Louis Federal Reserve.

0.80 €/$. The expected time-1 FX price of the euro is $E(X_1^{\$/€}) = (1.25\ \$/€)$ $(1.02) = 1.275\ \$/€$, whereas the expected time-1 FX price of the U.S. dollar is $E(X_1^{€/\$}) = (0.80\ €/\$)(1 - 0.01) = 0.792\ €/\$$. Exhibit 6.1 shows volatility estimates for some currencies.

Assume the time-0 spot FX rate for the New Zealand dollar is 0.80 $/NZ$, the expected time-1 spot FX rate is 0.776 $/NZ$, and the volatility of the NZ$ is 0.13.

(a) Find the expected rate of FX change in the NZ$.

(b) Use equation (6.2) to help find the approximate expected time-1 spot FX price of the U.S. dollar in terms of the NZ$.

Answers: (a) The expected rate of FX change of the NZ$ is $E(x^{\$/NZ\$}) =$ $(0.776\ \$/NZ\$)/(0.80\ \$/NZ\$) - 1 = -0.03$. (b) Equation (6.2) says that the expected rate of FX change of the U.S. dollar, relative to the NZ$, is approximately equal to $-(-0.03) + 0.13^2 = 0.0469$, or 4.69%. The expected time-1 FX price of the U.S. dollar, $E(X_1^{NZ\$/\$})$, is equal to $(1.25\ NZ\$/\$)(1.0469) = 1.309\ NZ\$/\$$.

UIRP, APPP, and Real Rates of Interest

As you know, the APPP and UIRP conditions are two prominent approaches to intrinsic FX rates. Economists believe that the actual FX rates are likely to be consistent with the APPP condition "in the long run," but violate the APPP condition "in the short run." A natural question to ask is whether the short-run APPP violations are related to the influence of the asset markets through the UIRP condition.

In this section we show how a currency can be overvalued relative to the APPP FX rate if the following conditions hold: (a) The APPP condition is expected to hold for N years from now. (b) The currency has the higher *real rate of interest*. For a country, the real rate of interest is the nominal rate of interest adjusted by the inflation rate. The U.S. real rate of interest, denoted $\rho^\$$, is thus the nominal rate of interest in U.S. dollars, $r^\$$, adjusted for the U.S. inflation rate, $p^\$$. Approximately, the real rate of interest is simply the nominal rate of interest minus the inflation rate, as shown in equation (6.3a). More precisely, the real rate of interest is given in equation (6.3b).

Real Rate of Interest

Linear Approximation

$$\rho^{\$} = r^{\$} - p^{\$} \qquad (6.3a)$$

Precise

$$1 + \rho^{\$} = (1 + r^{\$})/(1 + p^{\$}) \qquad (6.3b)$$

For example, assume that in the United States, the nominal rate of interest is 3.5% and the inflation rate is 2.5%. Then the real rate of interest is approximately $r^{\$} - p^{\$} = 3.5\% - 2.5\% = 1\%$, and is precisely $1.035/1.025 - 1 = 0.00976$, or 0.976%, which is almost 1%.

Assume that in the Eurozone, the nominal rate of interest is 5% and the inflation rate is 3%. What is the real rate of interest, using both the approximation and precise approaches?

Answers: Approximately $r^{\epsilon} - p^{\epsilon} = 5\% - 3\% = 2\%$, and precisely $1.05/1.03 - 1 = 0.0194$, or 1.94%, which is almost 2%.

Given long-run inflation rates of $p^{\yen}$ and $p^{\$}$ for Japan and the United States, respectively, the expected spot FX rate for time N is the APPP spot FX rate for time N found using the RPPP condition: $E(X_N^{\yen/\$}) = X_{PN}^{\yen/\$} = X_{P0}^{\yen/\$}[(1 + p^{\yen})/(1 + p^{\$})]^N$. For example, assume that today's price for the representative good in the United States is $100 and in Japan is ¥10,000. So today's APPP spot FX rate is $X_{P0}^{\yen/\$} = 100$ ¥/$. Assume that the long-term inflation rate for the United States is 2.5% and the long-term inflation rate for Japan is 1%. Assume arbitrarily that $N = 20$ years. So, $E(X_{20}^{\yen/\$}) = X_{P20}^{\yen/\$} = 100$ ¥/$[1.01/1.025]^{20} = 74.46$ ¥/$.

Assume further that the annualized long-term (20-year) nominal interest rates are 3.5% in U.S. dollars and 1.5% in yen. We use equation (5.1) to find the UIRP intrinsic spot FX rate, such that 74.46 ¥/$ = $X_{U0}^{\yen/\$}(1.015/1.035)^{20}$, which implies that today's intrinsic spot FX rate with the UIRP condition is $X_{U0}^{\yen/\$} = 110$ ¥/$. Given that the APPP condition is forecasted to hold at time N, and given that the UIRP condition holds today, the time-0 short-run intrinsic spot FX rate is 110 ¥/$. If today's actual spot FX rate is equal to 110 ¥/$, we say that the yen/U.S. dollar FX rate is currently correctly valued in the financial market, but misvalued in the goods market, where the U.S. dollar is overvalued and the yen is undervalued, given the time-0 APPP spot FX rate of 100 ¥/$.

In our example, the U.S. real rate of interest is approximately $r^\$ - p^\$ =$ 3.5% − 2.5% = 1%, and is precisely 0.976%. The U.S. real rate of interest is higher than the Japanese real rate of interest, $\rho^\yen$, which is approximately $r^\yen - p^\yen = 1.5\% - 1\% = 0.5\%$, and is precisely 0.495%. That the currency that is overvalued given the APPP condition, the U.S. dollar in our example, has the higher real rate of interest is no accident. Equation (6.4) shows how the two real rates of interest drive the ratio of time-0 intrinsic spot FX rates under the UIRP and APPP conditions, given that the APPP condition is expected to hold at time N.[4]

UIRP, APPP, and Real Interest Rates

$$X_{U0}^{\yen/\$}/X_{P0}^{\yen/\$} = [(1 + \rho^\$)/(1 + \rho^\yen)]^N \qquad (6.4)$$

For our example above, using the precise real rates of interest, the right-hand side of equation (6.4) is $(1.00495/1.00976)^{20} = 0.909$. The left-hand side of equation (6.4) is (100 ¥/$)/(110 ¥/$) = 0.909

So we see that if the two countries' real rates of interest are not equal, the currency with the higher real rate of interest has a higher short-run (UIRP) intrinsic spot FX value than long-run (APPP) intrinsic spot FX value. For example, if the U.S. dollar has a higher real rate of interest, then the U.S. dollar has a higher intrinsic spot FX value with the UIRP condition than with the APPP condition, because $X_{U0}^{\yen/\$} > X_{P0}^{\yen/\$}$. If the time-0 actual spot FX rate is equal to the time-0 UIRP intrinsic spot FX rate, the currency with the higher real rate of interest will be overvalued at time 0 from the perspective of the goods market and the APPP condition.

Assume that the annualized 20-year interest rate is 3.5% in U.S. dollars and 5% in euros, and that the inflation rate is 2.5% in the United States and 3% in the Eurozone. Assume the expected APPP spot FX rate for 20 years from now is 1.40 $/€.

(a) Find the time-0 UIRP spot FX rate, given the 20-year FX forecast.

(b) Show that the euro real rate of interest is higher than the U.S. dollar real rate of interest.

(c) Show that if the UIRP condition holds, the euro is overvalued relative to the time-0 APPP spot FX rate.

Answers: (a) Using equation (5.1) we find that $X_{U0}^{\$/€} = 1.87$ \$/€, since 1.40 \$/€ $= X_{U0}^{\$/€}(1.035/1.05)^{20}$. (b) The euro real rate of interest is $5\% - 3\% = 2\%$, whereas the U.S. dollar real rate of interest is $3.5\% - 2.5\% = 1\%$. (c) The time-0 APPP spot FX rate is found with 1.40 \$/€ $= X_{P0}^{\$/€}(1.025/1.03)^{20}$, so today's APPP spot FX rate is 1.54 \$/€. If the UIRP condition holds, so that the actual spot FX rate is equal to the UIRP FX rate, 1.87 \$/€, the euro is overvalued at time 0 relative to the APPP spot FX rate, 1.54 \$/€.

If the two countries' real rates of interest are equal, the UIRP condition yields the same time-0 intrinsic spot FX rate as the APPP condition. The equality of real rates of interest is an implicit assumption of the Fisher approach to how interest rate changes affect FX rates that we covered earlier. That is, if the interest rate of a country changes, the inflation rate of that country must also change in such a way as to maintain the equality of the two countries' real rates of interest. The result of the change in the inflation rate is a new forecasted FX rate, whereas the spot FX rate stays the same at the given APPP FX value.

The impact of real interest rate differentials on FX values is interesting but not easy to apply. The reason is that real interest rates are difficult to estimate, because inflation rates are difficult to forecast. Exhibit 6.2 shows selected historical real rates of interest compiled by the World Bank. Look at the real rate of interest estimates for the United States and the United Kingdom. Clearly, the historical estimates of $\rho^{\$}$ have been higher than those of $\rho^{£}$. So, applying the theory of this section, the British pound should be undervalued (relative to the U.S. dollar), based on purchasing power. Next, look at Brazil's very high real interest rates in Exhibit 6.2. The theory is that Brazil's currency will be overvalued based on purchasing power. The Big Mac Index in Chapter 3 showed the Brazilian real to be very overvalued based on purchasing power, especially after adjusting for Brazil's low GDP per capita.

Exhibit 6.2. Historical Real Rates of Interest

	2007	2008	2009	2010
Argentina	−2.8	0.3	5.2	−4.2
Australia	3.0	4.3	1.0	
Brazil	35.8	35.9	36.8	30.4
Chile	3.1	13.0	4.3	−8.4
China	−0.1	−2.3	5.9	−0.7
Colombia	9.8	8.7	8.5	6.1
Costa Rica	3.1	3.0	10.7	8.6
Hungary	3.5	4.7	7.2	4.4
Iceland	12.9	7.4	9.9	3.1
India	6.9	6.2	4.3	
Indonesia	2.3	−3.9	5.7	4.8
Italy	3.7	4.0	2.4	3.4
Japan	2.6	2.9	2.1	3.8
Korea, Rep.	4.4	4.1	2.1	1.7
Malaysia	1.4	−3.9	12.9	−0.1
Mexico	1.8	2.2	3.0	0.9
Netherlands	2.7	2.4	2.4	0.4
New Zealand	3.5	5.4	4.9	
Norway	4.2	−2.2	10.4	
Pakistan	3.8	−2.8	−4.5	1.9
Peru	20.5	22.8	18.5	11.3
Philippines	5.4	1.1	5.6	3.3
Russian Federation	−3.3	−4.9	13.1	−0.5
South Africa	4.7	5.7	4.2	1.6
Sri Lanka	2.7	2.2	9.2	2.7
Switzerland	0.6	0.9	2.6	2.7
Thailand	3.5	3.0	3.9	2.2
United Kingdom	2.5	1.6	−0.8	−2.4
United States	5.0	2.8	1.4	2.4

Source: World Bank.

Summary Action Points

- The UIRP condition is useful in estimating the expected rate of short-run intrinsic FX change, which in turn is useful in international finance applications.
- The two workhorse approaches of how interest rate changes affect FX rates are the asset market approach and the Fisher approach. These two approaches are differentiated from one another by the role of inflation.
- Siegel's paradox is a minor mathematical problem for the UIRP theory, based on the idea that the reciprocal of a mean cannot ever be equal to the mean of a reciprocal.
- The short-run (UIRP) intrinsic spot FX value of a currency will be higher than the long-run (APPP) intrinsic spot FX value of the currency, if the currency's economy has the higher real rate of interest.

Glossary

Expected rate of short-run intrinsic FX change: The expected percentage change in a currency, given that the currency is correctly valued in the financial markets.

Asset market approach: Changes in interest rates are not the result of changes in expected inflation rates and thus result in changes in current spot FX rates.

Fisher approach: Changes in interest rates reflect changes in anticipated inflation rates and therefore result in changes in expected future FX rates.

Real rate of interest: Approximately, the nominal interest rate minus the rate of inflation.

Siegel's paradox: The mathematical result that the expected future spot FX price of currency A relative to currency B is not equal to the reciprocal of the expected future spot FX price of currency B relative to currency A.

Discussion Questions

1. Explain the difference in the reaction of the FX market to (a) an interest rate change driven by a change in inflation expectation, and (b) an interest rate change driven by increased asset returns but no inflation change.

2. If the real rate of interest of Country A is higher than the real rate of interest in Country B, then in purchasing power terms, the currency of Country A will be overvalued relative to the currency of Country B. Evaluate this statement.

3. Explain the idea of Siegel's paradox.

Problems

1. Assume the one-year interest rates for the U.S. dollar and the euro are 3% and 5%, respectively. You expect a spot FX rate of 1.54 $/€ for a year from now. The spot FX rate today is 1.40 $/€. (a) Use the linear approximation UIRP condition to estimate the expected rate of change in the short-run intrinsic FX price of the euro. (b) What is the actual expected rate of change of the FX price of the euro?

2. Assume that the actual spot FX rate for the British pound is 1.50 $/£, the 1-year U.S. dollar interest rate is currently 3%, and the 1-year sterling interest rate is currently 5%. Assume that the 1-year U.S. dollar interest rate suddenly and unexpectedly rises to 4%, and all else stays the same. (a) Use the UIRP condition to determine the new spot FX rate for the pound, if the increase in the U.S. dollar interest rate is driven by the expectation of higher U.S. inflation. (b) What is the new expected percentage change in the FX price of the British pound?

3. Assume that the actual spot FX rate for the British pound is 1.50 $/£, the 1-year U.S. dollar interest rate is currently 3%, and the 1-year sterling interest rate is currently 5%. Assume that the 1-year U.S. dollar interest rate suddenly and unexpectedly rises to 4%, and all else stays the same. (a) Use the UIRP condition to determine the new spot FX rate for the pound, if the increase in the U.S. dollar interest rate is driven by higher U.S. short-term asset rates of return. (b) What is the new expected percentage change in the FX price of the British pound?

4. Assume that the actual spot FX rate for the British pound is 1.60 $/£, the one-year U.S. dollar interest rate is currently 8%, and the one-year sterling interest rate is currently 5%. Assume that the one-year U.S. dollar interest rate unexpectedly rises to 10%, and all else stays

the same. Use the UIRP condition to determine the new spot FX rate for the pound, if the increase in the U.S. dollar interest rate is (a) driven by the expectation of higher U.S. inflation, and (b) driven by higher U.S. short-term asset returns.

5. The spot FX rate is 1.24 $/€ today. At time 0 (now), the one-year interest rate for euros is 5% and for U.S. dollars is 3%. The expected spot FX rate a year from now is 1.22 $/€. The U.S. dollar interest rate unexpectedly drops to 2.5%, but there is no change in inflation expectations. What will be the new spot FX rate under the UIRP condition?

6. The spot FX rate is 1.24 $/€ today. At time 0 (now), the one-year interest rate for euros is 5%, and for U.S. dollars is 3%. The expected spot FX rate a year from now is 1.22 $/€. The U.S. dollar interest rate unexpectedly drops to 2.5%, due to a drop in inflation expectations in the United States. What will be the new spot FX rate under the UIRP condition?

7. Refer to #5. (a) What is the new expected rate of change in the FX price of the euro, using the linear approximation of the UIRP condition? (b) Compare the linear approximation in (a) to the true expected rate of change in the FX price of the euro.

8. Refer to #6. (a) What is the new expected rate of change in the FX price of the euro, using the linear approximation of the UIRP condition? (b) Compare the linear approximation in (a) to the true expected rate of change in the FX price of the euro.

9. There is a 50% chance that the spot FX rate for a year from now will be 0.625 $/€ and a 50% chance that it will be 1.25 $/€. What is the expected spot FX rate for a year from now? What is the expected spot FX price of the U.S. dollar? Show Siegel's paradox.

10. Assume the British pound is expected to appreciate by 3% relative to the U.S. dollar over the next year, the time-0 spot FX rate is 1.60 $/£, and the volatility of the British pound is 0.09. (a) Find the expected time-1 spot FX price of the British pound. (b) Use equation (6.2) to help find the approximate expected time-1 spot FX price of the U.S. dollar in terms of the British pound.

11. Assume the annualized interest rate for 10-year fixed income assets in U.S. dollars is 4%, whereas the annualized interest rate for 10-year

fixed income assets in British pounds is 6%. Assume that the inflation rate in the United States is 3.5% and the inflation rate in the United Kingdom is 4.5%. Assume today's APPP spot FX rate is 1.50 $/£. Assume the APPP condition holds in the long run (10 years from now). (a) Find the spot FX rate for today that is consistent with the UIRP condition. (b) Show that the real rate of interest in British pounds is higher than the real rate of interest in U.S. dollars. (c) Show that if UIRP condition holds, the British pound is overvalued relative to today's APPP spot FX value.

Answers to Problems

1. (a) 3% − 5% = −2%.
   (b) (1.54 $/€)/(1.40 $/€) − 1 = 0.10, or 10%.
2. (a) No change, 1.50 $/£.
   (b) new $E(X_1^{\$/£})$ = 1.50 $/£(1.04/1.05) = 1.486 $/£; so 1.486/1.50 − 1
   = −0.0097, or −1%; Or, 4% − 5% = −1%.
3. (a) Old $E(X_1^{\$/£})$ = 1.50 $/£(1.03/1.05) = 1.47 $/£; 1.47 $/£ = new
   $X_{U0}^{\$/£}$(1.04/1.05) = 1.485 $/£.
   (b) 1.47/1.485 − 1 = −0.0097, or −1%; Or, 4% − 5% = −1%.
4. (a) 1.60 $/£;
   (b) 1.571 $/£. In part (b), you first find the expected spot FX rate for time 1. It is 1.60 $/£ (1.08/1.05) = 1.646 $/£. Then use that rate with the new $r^{\$}$ to find the new time-0 spot FX rate: 1.646 $/£/(1.10/1.05) = 1.571 $/£ .
5. The new spot FX rate, given financial market conditions and the market FX forecast, is $X_{U0}^{\$/€}$ in the equation, 1.22 $/€ = $X_{U0}^{\$/€}$ (1.025/1.05). So $X_{U0}^{\$/€}$ = 1.25 $/€.
6. Stays at 1.24 $/€ (Fisher approach).
7. (a) 0.025 − 0.05 = −0.025, or −2.5%.
   (b) (1.22 $/€)/(1.25 $/€) − 1 = −0.024, or −2.4%.
8. (a) 0.025 − 0.05 = −0.025, or −2.5%.
   (b) The new expected time-1 spot FX rate is (1.24 $/€)(1.025/1.05)
   = 1.21 $/€; (1.21 $/€)/(1.24 $/€) − 1 = −0.024, or −2.4%.
9. $E(X_1^{\$/€})$ = 0.9375 $/€; $E(X_1^{€/\$})$ = 1.20 €/$. Because 1/(0.9375 $/€) = 1.067 €/$, we see Siegel's paradox.

10. (a) The expected time-1 FX price of the British pound is $E(X_1^{\$/£})$ = (1.60 $/£)(1.03) = 1.648 $/£.

(b) Equation (6.2) says that the expected rate of change of the U.S. dollar, relative to the British pound, is approximately equal to $-0.03 + 0.09^2 = -0.0219$, or -2.19%. The expected time-1 FX price of the U.S. dollar is $E(X_1^{£/\$})$ = (0.625 £/$)(1 − 0.0219) = 0.6113 £/$.

11. (a) We first need to find the forecasted FX value of the British pound for time 10: 1.50 $/£$(1.035/1.045)^{10}$ = 1.36 $/£. Using that forecast for $E(X_{10}^{\$/£})$, we can use equation (5.1) to find the UIRP spot FX rate for time 0: 1.36 $/£ = $X_{U0}^{\$/£}(1.04/1.06)^{10}$, which implies that $X_{U0}^{\$/£}$ = 1.65 $/£.

(b) The real rate of interest in British pounds is (approximately) 6% − 4.5% = 1.5%, whereas the real rate of interest in U.S. dollars is (approximately) 4% − 3.5% = 0.5%.

(c) If the UIRP condition holds, so that the actual spot FX rate is equal to the UIRP intrinsic spot FX rate, 1.65 $/£, the British pound is currently overvalued relative to the APPP spot FX rate, 1.50 $/£.

CHAPTER 7

Forward FX Contracts

Forward foreign exchange (FX) contracts are used by many companies to help manage the risk posed by uncertain future FX rate fluctuations. This chapter covers some basics of forward FX contracts and forward FX rates. We'll encounter another version of interest rate parity, called the *covered interest rate parity (CIRP) condition*. As you will see, the CIRP condition looks deceptively similar to the traditional UIRP condition, so much so that some people confuse them, but the two relationships are conceptually very different. The UIRP condition we covered already is based on economic theory, while we will see that the CIRP condition is a different kind of relationship, called a financial no-arbitrage condition.

Forward FX Rates

In a *forward FX contract*, two parties contract today for the future exchange of currencies at a *forward FX rate*. No funds change hands when a typical forward FX contract originates; a funds flow occurs only at the contract's stated future delivery time. Like spot FX rates, forward FX rates vary constantly with market activity. Once a forward FX contract is made between two parties, the forward FX rate *for that contract* is set and does not change.

The FX market constantly sees an array of market-determined forward FX rates for various delivery horizons. In practice, forward FX rates are quoted for standard periods; one-month, three-month, six-month, and one-year contracts are the most common. But many banks quote forward FX rates for standard horizons up to 10 years for actively traded currencies. Participants in both the retail and interbank sectors of the FX market routinely make forward FX transactions. About 30% of forward FX transactions involve a nonfinancial customer, and are typically entered to allow the entity to manage FX risk.

Although forward FX quotes of the interbank market are obtainable via Bloomberg and other online financial services, it is not that easy to find quotes on the Internet. The quotes in Exhibit 7.1 for the Sf/$ on January 10, 2013, are from http://www.investing.com/rates-bonds/forward-rates. The site only quotes forward FX "points"; the forward FX rates shown in Exhibit 7.1 are based on the spot FX rates and the quoted forward FX points. For example, the ask spot FX rate, 0.9238 Sf/$, adjusted for the 5yr decimalized quoted forward FX points, –0.0568, yields the 5yr ask forward FX rate, 0.8670 Sf$.

The forward FX rate quotes in Exhibit 7.1 for the Sf/$ are expressed in conventional European terms. It may help to think here of the Swiss franc as the pricing currency and the U.S. dollar as a "commodity" in which a dealer (typically a bank) is making a market. Thus the one-year bid/ask quotes imply that a dealer is willing to buy one-year U.S. dollars at 0.9161 Sf/$ and sell one-year U.S. dollars at 0.9168 Sf/$. A trader seeking a one-year forward FX position on U.S. dollars may contract with the dealer to sell U.S. dollars at 0.9161 Sf/$ or buy U.S. dollars at 0.9168 Sf/$.

If a currency's forward FX price (not the FX rate, but the FX price of the currency) is *lower* than its current spot FX price, the currency is said to be at a *forward discount* (for that specific horizon). Similarly, if a currency's forward FX price is *higher* than its current spot FX price, the currency is said to be at a *forward premium*. Of course, for currencies that are conventionally quoted in European terms, like the Swiss franc, higher FX rate quotes mean lower FX prices of Swiss francs. Thus, in the FX rate quotes

Exhibit 7.1. Forward and Spot FX Quotes (Sf/$) January 10, 2013

| Expiration | Bid | | Ask | |
	FX rate	Points	FX rate	Points
Spot	0.9234		0.9238	
6 mo	0.9204	–30	0.9209	–29
1 yr	0.9161	–73	0.9168	–70
2 yr	0.9062	–172	0.9076	–162
5 yr	0.8631	–603	0.8670	–568

Source: http://www.investing.com/rates-bonds/forward-rates.

in Exhibit 7.1, the U.S. dollar is at a forward discount (relative to the Swiss franc), because the FX price of the U.S. dollar is lower in the forward FX market than in the spot FX market. The Swiss franc is correspondingly at a forward premium (relative to the U.S. dollar) for all future delivery times, because the FX price of the Swiss franc is higher in the forward FX market than in the spot FX market.

Forward FX contracts are often tailor-made to meet specific user needs. For example, a retail customer wanting a 73-day forward FX contract can get one from a bank. In principle, any two parties may create an informal forward FX contract for any delivery time in the future. In the FX market, forward FX contracts for nonmajor currencies, especially for longer forward horizons, are generally less liquid than for major currencies, resulting in wider dealer bid/ask spreads, and thus higher transaction fees for retail users. Spreads in the interbank market are substantially lower than in the retail market. Typically, we'll assume there is sufficient liquidity and ignore dealer bid/ask spreads.

The notation we use for a forward FX rate (using U.S. dollars and euros as representative currencies) is $F_N^{\$/€}$, where the subscript denotes the number of years until delivery. N may be a fraction of a year, including longer than one year (e.g., $N = 3.25$ is three years, three months.)

Long and Short Forward FX Positions

When one has possession of a commodity, one is sometimes said to be *long* the commodity, or have a *long position* in the commodity. Moreover, one is long something that is a receivable. Similarly, if one owes, or is obligated to deliver, a commodity, one is said to be *short* that commodity. All forward FX contracts involve two parties. If one contracts forward to buy euros with U.S. dollars, one is said to take a *long forward position in (or on) euros*, with the implicit understanding that the forward FX contract is denominated in terms of U.S. dollars. The other party in the forward FX agreement, with the obligation to deliver (or sell) euros, is said to take a *short forward position in (or on) euros*.

Analyzing forward FX contracts can at first be confusing, as a long position on one currency is a short position on the other currency. It is helpful to standardize the analysis by referring to a contract's *SIZE* (denoted Z) in units of the foreign currency (as if it were a commodity), and to the contract's *AMOUNT* (denoted A) in units of the pricing currency. The term *SIZE* is meant to convey the idea of physical volume, whereas the term *AMOUNT* conveys a monetary dimension. To prevent confusion, the pricing currency of our forward FX contracts will be U.S. dollars unless otherwise stated. Thus, for a forward FX contract on euros, the contract *SIZE* is expressed in euros with notation $Z^{€}$, whereas the contract *AMOUNT* is expressed in U.S. dollars with notation $A^{\$}$.

A forward FX contract's *SIZE* and *AMOUNT* are converted into each other at the forward FX rate: $A^{\$} = Z^{€}(F_N^{\$/€})$. For example, if $A^{\$}$ is $1,000 and the forward FX rate is 1.25 $/€, then $Z^{€} = \$1{,}000/(1.25 \ \$/€)$ = €800. This example contract obligates the long euro forward position to receive €800 and pay $1,000 one year after the contract is made. At time 1, the short euro position must deliver €800 and will receive $1,000. (As you can see, the short position on euros is the same as a long position on U.S. dollars, with the euro as the pricing currency.)

You take a one-year long forward position on Japanese yen at a forward FX rate of 108 ¥/$. State the cash flow obligations of your long forward position on yen, now and a year from now, if the contract *AMOUNT* ($A^{\$}$) is $1,000. What is the forward FX contract's *SIZE* ($Z^{¥}$)?

Answer: No cash flows now; a year from now, you receive ¥108,000 (the contract's *SIZE*) and deliver (pay) the contract's *AMOUNT*, $1,000.

You take a one-year short forward position on British pounds at a forward FX rate of 1.50 $/£. State the cash flow obligations of your short forward position on pounds, now and a year from now, if the contract *SIZE* is £150 million. What is the contract *AMOUNT*?

Answer: No cash flows now; a year from now, you pay £150 million and receive $225 million (the contract's *AMOUNT*).

A forward FX transaction is often part of an *FX swap*, which is the simultaneous *spot* sale (or purchase) of currency against a *forward* purchase (or sale) of approximately an equal amount. When not part of an FX swap, a forward FX transaction is often called an *outright forward*. The FX swap market has the highest daily volume of the FX market. In 2007, FX swap transactions accounted for $1.7 billion of the $3.2 billion daily FX market turnover. Spot FX transactions were about $1 billion, and the rest were outright FX forward transactions. FX swaps are usually very short-term contracts. The great majority have a maturity of less than one week. Financial institutions are the primary players in FX swap transactions.

Money market traders often use FX swaps to reduce exposure to short-term FX changes. Suppose a U.S. trader wants to invest in a seven-day British pound certificate of deposit (CD). The trader buys spot pounds, to use to purchase the CD, and simultaneously sells pounds forward in a single FX swap transaction. The FX swap transaction simultaneously provides the trader the funds to buy the CD and provides protection against a depreciation of the pound during the life of the CD.

Difference Check Settlement of a Forward FX Contract

There are two ways to settle a forward FX contract at the delivery time: The first is *gross settlement*, through physical exchange of the currencies per the contract. The second is *net settlement*, through a *difference check*. Both settlement methods are widely used.

Assume a one-year forward FX contract on euros with $A^\$ = \$1,000$ and a forward FX rate of 1.25 $/€; thus $Z^€ = €800$. With the gross settlement method, which we already covered, the long euro party receives €800 and pays $1,000. The short euro party pays €800 and receives $1,000. The spot FX rate at the delivery time is irrelevant in the gross settlement method.

With the net settlement method, there is a difference check based on the spot FX rate prevailing at the delivery time. Suppose the spot FX rate at the delivery time (a year from now in our contract) turns out to be $X_1^{\$/€}$ = 1.35 $/€, implying that the €800 that the short position on euros is scheduled to deliver would be *equivalent* at that time to €800(1.35 $/€) = $1,080. Because the long position on euros is scheduled to receive euros that would be worth $1,080 and to deliver $1,000, the long position's net monetary gain is $1,080 − $1,000 = $80.

Similarly, the short position on euros has a net loss of $80, because the party is scheduled to deliver euros worth $1,080 and receive $1,000. So the difference check settlement would be $80 (or equivalently, $80/(1.35 $/€) = €59.26), from the short position on euros to the long position on euros. If the long euro position wants the entire €800 for which it contracted, but the settlement is via difference check, the $1,000 that would have been physically delivered can instead be combined with the received difference check of $80 to buy $1,080/(1.35 $/€) = €800 in the spot FX market at the delivery time. Either way, through physical delivery or spot FX purchase at the delivery time (with the help of the difference check), the long position on euros ends up with €800 in our example. *The key advantage of the difference check approach is that it avoids the need for both parties to actually have the full funds for the settlement.*

The difference check is received by the long position on a currency if the currency's delivery time spot FX price is higher than the forward FX contract price. In the example, the delivery time spot FX price of the euro is higher at $X_1^{\$/€} = 1.35$ $/€ than $F_1^{\$/€} = 1.25$ $/€, so the long position on euros receives a difference check from the short position. If the spot FX price of the euro at the delivery time is lower than the contracted forward FX price, the short position on euros would receive the difference check from the long position on euros. For example, if the spot FX rate was $X_1^{\$/€} = 1.05$ $/€ at the delivery time, the spot FX price of the euro would thus be lower than the contracted forward FX price of the euro, 1.25 $/€. The U.S. dollar equivalent to €800 (the short euro position's obligated delivery) is €800(1.05 $/€) = $840. Thus, the long euro position would pay a difference check of $160 (= $1,000 − $840) to the short position on euros.

Using $ to denote the pricing currency, and € for the foreign currency, we can specify a formula to calculate the amount of the difference check (or net gain) at the delivery time, expressed in the pricing currency ($): *First, express the FX rates in direct terms from the point of view of the pricing currency* ($). Next, multiply the contract *SIZE* (in foreign currency units) by the difference between the actual delivery-time spot FX price of the foreign currency and the contract's forward FX price of the foreign currency. This calculation yields the difference check amount *from the perspective of the long* position on the foreign currency, denoted $D_€^{\$}$, as expressed in equation (7.1):

Forward FX Contract Difference Check Settlement

Long Position on Foreign Currency

$$D_{\epsilon}^{\$} = Z^{\epsilon}(X_N^{\$/\epsilon} - F_N^{\$/\epsilon}) \qquad (7.1)$$

Remember that the *super*script symbol denotes the currency in which a security or contract is priced (or denominated), whereas the *sub*script symbol denotes the currency to which the contract is exposed. So in $D_{\epsilon}^{\$}$, the U.S. dollar is the pricing currency, whereas the euro is the currency to which the forward contract is exposed. Using equation (7.1) in our first example with $F_1^{\$/\epsilon} = 1.25$ $/€, if $X_1^{\$/\epsilon} = 1.35$ $/€, the long position on euros would receive $D_{\epsilon}^{\$} = €800(1.35\ \$/\epsilon - 1.25\ \$/\epsilon) = \$80$. In the second example, where $X_1^{\$/\epsilon} = 1.05$ $/€, the long position on euros would receive $D_{\epsilon}^{\$} = €800(1.05\ \$/\epsilon - 1.25\ \$/\epsilon) = -\$160$. The negative amount indicates that the long euro position would pay this amount to the short euro position. The next example applies equation (7.1) with European terms FX rate quotes.

You take a short position in a (U.S. dollar priced) forward FX contract on Japanese yen at a forward FX rate of $F_1^{\yen/\$} = 120$ ¥/$. The contract *AMOUNT* is $1 million. If the spot FX rate at delivery time is $X_1^{\yen/\$} = 100$ ¥/$, what is your gain (loss) in U.S. dollars on the short yen forward position?

Answer: The contract *SIZE* is $1 million (120 ¥/$) = ¥120 million. To apply equation (7.1), the European terms quotes must be reciprocated into direct terms from the U.S. dollar point of view. The U.S. dollar gain for the long yen position in the forward FX contract, using equation (7.1), is ¥120 million[1/(100 ¥/$) − 1/(120 ¥/$)] = ¥120 million [0.01 $/¥ − 0.00833 $/¥] = $200,000. Because the gain to the long position is $200,000, your short position loses $200,000.

The difference check may also be interpreted as the net profit (loss) on a forward FX position. Figure 7.1 shows the net profit (loss) on forward FX positions on euros as a function of the delivery time spot FX rate.

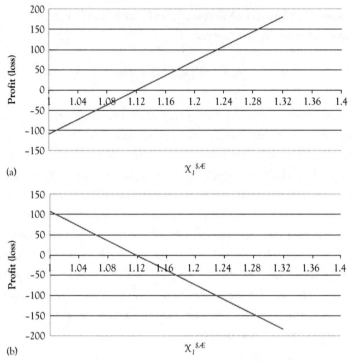

(a)

(b)

Figure 7.1. Net profit and loss for forward FX positions on euros. (a) Profit (loss) on a LONG forward FX position on euros as a function of the delivery time (time-1) spot FX price of the euro. This is the same as the difference check settlement to the long forward FX position. (b) Profit (loss) on a SHORT forward FX position on euros as a function of the delivery time (time-1) spot FX price of the euro. This is the same as the difference check settlement to the short forward FX position.

Synthetic FX Forwards

Suppose you conduct three simultaneous transactions, all at time 0: (a) Take out a one-year U.S. dollar loan with time-0 proceeds of $100; at an interest rate of $r^\$ = 10\%$; the time-1 face value of the loan is thus $100(1.10) = $110. (b) FX the $100 loan proceeds into Swiss francs at an assumed current spot FX rate of $X_0^{Sf/\$} = 1.50$ Sf/$, to get $100(1.50 Sf/\$) = Sf 150. (c) Put the Sf 150 into a one-year Swiss franc deposit yielding $r^{Sf} = 8\%$.

Together, the three transactions are sometimes called a *cash-and-carry strategy*. The cash-and-carry deal involves no *net* cash flow into or out of your pocket at the time of the three simultaneous transactions, time 0. But a year from now, you will receive Sf 150(1.08) = Sf 162 from the liqui-dation of the Swiss franc deposit, and you will have to repay the $110 face value on the U.S. dollar loan. Thus, at time 1, there is an inflow to you of Sf 162 and an outflow from you of $110. This inflow/outflow is the same as if you held a long position in an *actual* one-year forward FX contract on Swiss francs, with a contract *AMOUNT* of $110 and a contract *SIZE* of Sf 162. So the cash-and-carry deal has an implicit forward FX rate of Sf 162/$110 = 1.473 Sf/$.

In financial markets, a security or instrument that is engineered from other securities or instruments combined is termed a *synthetic*. The three transactions of your cash-and-carry deal represent a synthetic long forward FX position on Swiss francs. The implicit forward FX rate is called the synthetic forward FX rate. Of course, the carry trades you learned about in Chapter 5 are examples of synthetic forward FX positions. For a dia-gram of the process of creating a synthetic long forward FX position on Swiss francs with the cash-and-carry strategy, see Figure 7.2. We use Y to denote "synthetic," in the forward FX rate notation.

You could create a synthetic *short* forward FX position by reversing the direction of the three simultaneous time-0 cash-and-carry transactions. First, borrow Sf 150 for one year at r^{Sf} = 8%, so that Sf 162 will be repaid at time 1. Next, FX the borrowed Sf 150 into U.S. dollars at time 0 at the assumed spot FX rate of $X_0^{Sf/\$}$ = 1.50 Sf/$, to get $100. Finally, place the $100 at time 0 into a one-year deposit at the U.S. dollar interest rate of

		Date		
		0		1
Currency				
U.S. dollars	Borrow $100	x (1 + 0.10)		Repay $110
	⇓			
	$X_0^{Sf/\$}$ = 1.50 Sf/$		$F_{Y1}^{Sf/\$}$ = Sf 162/$110 = 1.473 Sf/$	
	⇓			
Swiss francs	Deposit Sf 150	x (1 + 0.08)		Receive Sf 162

Figure 7.2. Cash-and-carry strategy. Synthetic one-year long FX for-ward position on Swiss francs: (a) borrow US dollars for one year; (b) spot exchange the US dollars into Swiss francs; (c) deposit the Swiss francs for one year.

$r^\$$ = 10%, to end up with \$110 at time 1. In effect, you have created a contract that involves no *net* cash flow (into or out of your pocket) at time 0, but it obligates you to pay Sf 162 and receive \$110 at time 1. Thus, you have manufactured a synthetic short one-year forward FX position on Swiss francs with a synthetic forward FX rate of Sf 162/\$110 = 1.473 Sf/\$.

At time 0 you borrow \$1,000 in time-1 face value for one year at a 6% U.S. dollar interest rate ($r^\$$), FX the borrowed proceeds into British pounds at the spot FX rate of $X_0^{\$/\pounds}$ = 1.60 \$/£, and place the British pounds in a one-year deposit at $r^\pounds$ = 8%. How many British pounds will you receive from your sterling deposit at time 1, and what is the synthetic forward FX rate?

Answers: The time-0 proceeds from the U.S. dollar loan are \$1,000/1.06 = \$943.40, which FXs to \$943.40/(1.60 \$/£) = £589.62. The time-1 liquidation of the sterling deposit is £589.62(1.08) = £636.79. The synthetic forward FX rate is \$1,000/£636.79 = 1.57 \$/£.

You can use a memory device to prompt your understanding of a synthetic forward FX position: *The direction of the spot FX transaction in the cash-and-carry (synthetic) strategy is the same as in the forward FX position you are synthetically creating.* Once you know the direction of the spot FX transaction of the synthetic, the loan/deposit directions fall into place. Thus, a synthetic *long* forward FX position on Swiss francs involves a *purchase* of Swiss francs. Because you need U.S. dollars to buy the Swiss francs in the spot FX market for the cash-and-carry deal, you therefore know that you must *borrow* U.S. dollars; and after the spot FX purchase, you have Swiss francs, which you must deposit. For a mental check, you can think that at the delivery time, you will receive the Swiss francs as proceeds from the deposit and pay U.S. dollars to repay the loan, the same basic delivery time cash flows in an actual long forward FX position on Swiss francs.

Synthetic *LONG* forward FX position on Swiss francs:

1. Borrow U.S. dollars
2. Spot FX the proceeds to Swiss francs
3. Deposit the Swiss francs

Synthetic *SHORT* forward FX position on Swiss francs:

1. Borrow Swiss francs
2. Spot FX the proceeds to U.S. dollars
3. Deposit the U.S. dollars

Using a Y subscript to denote "synthetic," the synthetic forward FX rate can be computed directly via equation (7.2):

Synthetic Forward FX Rate

$$F_{YN}^{Sf/\$} = X_0^{Sf/\$}[(1 + r^{Sf})/(1 + r^{\$})]^N \qquad (7.2)$$

For example, using the assumptions in the example above where $N = 1$, equation (7.2) yields that the synthetic forward FX rate, $F_{Y1}^{Sf/\$}$, is equal to 1.50 Sf/$(1.08/1.10) = 1.473 Sf/$. Note that once again, just as in the style of the RPPP and UIRP conditions, if the "future" FX rate is on the left-hand side, the "numerator" interest rate is for the "numerator" currency of the FX rate.

Assume the one-year U.S. dollar interest rate is 6%, the one-year British pound interest rate is 8%, and the spot FX rate is $X_0^{\$/£} = 1.60$ $/£. What is the synthetic forward FX rate using equation (7.2)?

Answer: (1.60 $/£)(1.06/1.08) = 1.57 $/£.

Why would anyone want to construct a synthetic forward FX position instead of simply using an actual forward FX position? The answer is if the synthetic forward FX rate is better than the actual forward FX rate (considering transaction costs). For example, suppose the actual one-year forward FX rate is 1.46 Sf/$ and the synthetic forward FX rate is 1.47 Sf/$. If you want a long forward position on Swiss francs, which would be more advantageous, the actual FX forward or the synthetic FX forward? The answer is whichever position allows the forward purchase of Swiss francs at the better FX rate, that is, at the lower FX price of the Swissie. Thus, the synthetic should be the choice for a long forward FX position on Swiss francs, rather than the actual FX forward. If you want to establish a short forward FX position on Swiss francs, the better choice would be via the *actual* forward FX contract, not a synthetic short forward FX position. The reason is that it is better to sell Swiss francs at 1.46 Sf/$ than at 1.47 Sf/$.

Assume that presently the spot FX rate is 1.80 $/£ and that the actual 1-year forward FX rate is 1.75 $/£. The one-year U.S. dollar interest rate is 3%; the one-year pound sterling interest rate is 7%.

(a) What is the synthetic one-year forward FX rate?

(b) Which is better if you want to take a one-year short forward FX position on British pounds, an actual forward FX contract or a synthetic one?

Answers: (a) (1.80 $/£)(1.03/1.07) = 1.733 $/£; (b) it is better to sell pounds forward at the actual forward FX rate of 1.75 $/£ than at the synthetic rate of 1.733 $/£.

Covered Interest Rate Parity

Unless the actual forward FX rate equals the synthetic forward FX rate, a financial arbitrage opportunity is available. If no arbitrage opportunity is available, the actual forward FX rate is equal to the synthetic forward FX rate. Using equation (7.2), we get an equality is referred to as the *CIRP condition*, equation (7.3).

Covered Interest Rate Parity

$$F_N^{Sf/\$} = X_0^{Sf/\$}[(1 + r^{Sf})/(1 + r^{\$})]^N \qquad (7.3)$$

For the Swiss franc example, given the spot FX rate of $X_0^{Sf/\$} = 1.50$ Sf/$, $r^{Sf} = 8\%$, and $r^{\$} = 10\%$, equation (7.3) shows that the actual forward FX rate should be (1.50 Sf/$)(1.08/1.10) = 1.473 Sf/$, or else there is an arbitrage opportunity. As before, equation (7.3) is expressed with the forward FX rate on the left-hand side of the equation. Under this arrangement, *the interest rates in the numerator and denominator should match the "numerator" and "denominator" currency symbols in the superscript of the FX quote.*

	Date		
	0		1
Currency			
U.S. dollars	$1	$x(1 + r^\$)$	$= \$1(1 + r^\$)$
	$X_0^{Sf/\$}$		$F_1^{Sf/\$} = X_0^{Sf/\$}(1 + r^{Sf})/(1 + r^\$)$
Swiss francs	$X_0^{Sf/\$}$	$x(1 + r^{Sf})$	$= X_0^{Sf/\$}(1 + r^{Sf})$

Figure 7.3. Covered interest rate parity.

When the synthetic forward FX price of the Swiss franc is too high, in comparison to the actual forward FX price, arbitrageurs will buy Swiss francs in the actual forward FX market and sell Swiss francs in the spot FX market (in the synthetic transactions of the cash-and-carry strategy) to capture the arbitrage opportunity. This buying low-selling high pushes the spot FX price of the Swiss franc lower and the forward FX price higher, until the arbitrage opportunity is eliminated, and equation (7.3) holds with actual spot and forward FX rates. Figure 7.3 displays a diagram of the CIRP relation.

It would be nice for us readers to be the only ones to understand the CIRP condition and how to put on the arbitrage strategy. But both the CIRP condition and the arbitrage strategy are well known in FX markets. Moreover, the arbitrage is relatively easy and inexpensive for interbank FX traders in many cases. For these reasons, one would expect FX market traders to pounce on even minor deviations from the CIRP condition, and the arbitrage trading would cause the deviation to quickly disappear. Thus the CIRP condition tends to hold very closely and continuously, at least for major liquid currencies. Indeed, empirical testing of equation (7.3) for actively traded currencies of developed countries confirms that the CIRP condition is very accurate. All that said, CIRP violations occurred during some of the most chaotic days of the global financial crisis in 2008. And there are times when there are apparent arbitrage opportunities in the currencies of less-developed countries. One example is explained in the Northstar Mexican Peso Arbitrage box.

Northstar Mexican Peso Arbitrage

In mid-1993, the multinational company Northstar arbitraged the forward FX market between U.S. dollars and Mexican pesos. Northstar borrowed U.S. dollars from its lead commercial bank at the prime interest rate of 6%, spot-FXed the U.S. dollars into pesos at the spot FX rate of 3.11 Pe/$, and then invested the proceeds into peso-denominated Mexican government bills yielding about 16%. Effectively, Northstar used this cash-and-carry strategy to create a *synthetic* long forward FX position on pesos. That is, if Northstar borrowed $1,000, spot-FXed into Pe 3,110, and deposited the Pe 3,110 for a year at 16%, it would end up with Pe 3,110(1.16) = Pe 3,607.50 and an obligation to repay $1,000(1.06) = $1,060. This strategy represents a synthetic long forward FX position on pesos with a synthetic forward FX rate of (3.11 Pe/$)(1.16/1.06) = 3.40 Pe/$.

Northstar's bank was quoting an *actual* forward FX rate at a lower forward discount than represented by the synthetic forward FX rate. Say, for example, that the actual forward FX rate quote was 3.30 Pe/$. Northstar was covering its long synthetic forward positions on pesos (at 3.40 Pe/$) by going short actual forward FX contracts on pesos (at 3.30 Pe/$). Northstar was thus practicing a form of covered interest arbitrage by selling pesos forward (actually) at 3.30 Pe/$ while simultaneously buying them forward (synthetically) at 3.40 Pe/$.

The arbitrage was made possible when the Mexican government attempted to support the spot FX price of the peso via a high peso interest rate. The market then quoted a low-discount actual forward FX price of the peso in the expectation that the peso would not depreciate to the extent implicit in the interest rates in the synthetic forward FX rate. This kind of arbitrage is generally not available in the market for FX of developed countries that do not try to control their currency values.[1]

The Forward FX Rate as a Forecast

The CIRP condition is so deceptively similar to the UIRP condition, that some people mistake them as the same thing. But the two relationships are very different. The CIRP condition is a financial no-arbitrage condition, and tends to hold in the real world for developed country currencies, because the financial arbitrage to enforce it is relatively easy. In contrast, the UIRP condition is a theory that cannot be enforced by financial arbitrage, so it is much easier for the UIRP condition not to hold in the real world.

Given the CIRP condition, if the UIRP condition does hold, the forward FX rate is equal to the expected future spot FX rate, $F_N^{S/\$} = E(X_N^{S/\$})$. Because of this logic, many economists refer to the empirical evidence against the UIRP condition as the "forward premium puzzle." (Note also that Siegel's paradox (Chapter 6) is an issue. Because we know that $F_N^{\$/Sf} = 1/F_N^{S/\$}$, but $E(X_N^{\$/Sf}) \neq 1/E(X_N^{S/\$})$, the forward FX rate can technically be equal to the expected spot FX rate in only one currency direction, at most.)

It is tempting to regard the forward FX rate as the "market's" forecast of the future spot FX rate. If you use the forward FX rate as a forecast, you may not realize that you are implicitly assuming that the traditional UIRP condition holds. But we just used the term *forward premium puzzle* to name the large body of empirical evidence that the forward FX rate is **not** a good forecast for the future spot FX rate. So using the forward FX rate as a forecast does not seem like the best approach, despite how good the idea sounds. Note also that we saw bank forecasts in Chapter 5 that differed from the expected spot FX rates under the UIRP condition, and therefore differed from forward FX rates. If the best forecast is an APPP FX rate, the forward FX rate will not generally be equal to that forecast either.

Indeed, traders who use the forward FX rate as a forecast would not engage in the fundamental analysis and trading that is supposed to enforce the UIRP condition. So the more that traders use the forward FX rate as their FX forecast, the less is the theoretical basis for the UIRP condition. That is, the forward FX rate can only be equal to the expected spot FX rate if enough traders make informed speculative trades using FX forecasts based on fundamental economic factors, not using the forward FX rate itself as the forecast.

Covered Interest Arbitrage

In this section we show in more detail the arbitrage strategy for capturing deviations from the CIRP condition, called *covered interest arbitrage*. For example, assume (a) the one-year interest rates are $r^{Sf} = 8\%$ and $r^{\$} = 10\%$; (b) the spot FX rate is 1.50 Sf/$; and (c) the actual one-year forward FX rate is $F_1^{Sf/\$} = 1.46$ Sf/$. The CIRP condition does not hold, and an arbitrage profit is possible, because the actual forward FX rate is not equal to the synthetic one-year forward FX rate, $X_0^{Sf/\$}[(1 + r^{Sf})/(1 + r^{\$})] = 1.50$ Sf/$ $(1.08/1.10) = 1.473$ Sf/$. In a covered interest arbitrage strategy, you take an actual forward FX position in one direction, and then counterbalance with a synthetic forward position in the other direction. To see how to do this in our example, note that today's actual forward FX rate of 1.46 Sf/$ is a *higher* FX price of the Swiss franc than the synthetic forward FX rate of 1.473 Sf/$. You want to "buy low and sell high." Thus your arbitrage strategy will involve going short on Swiss francs at the actual forward FX rate of 1.46 Sf/$ and simultaneously going long on Swiss francs at the synthetic forward FX rate of 1.473 Sf/$.

The synthetic long Swiss franc position is the cash-and-carry strategy of borrowing U.S. dollars, using them to buy Swiss francs at the current spot FX rate, and then depositing the Swiss francs. You are going to do this in such a way as to be able to extract the arbitrage profit at time 0. Taking an actual short forward position on Swiss francs with a contract *SIZE* of Sf 1.46, will obligate you to deliver Sf 1.46 and receive $1.00 a year from now. So you need a synthetic long forward position on Swiss francs that will give you Sf 1.46 a year from now to deliver against the actual forward FX position. That is, you will need to end up with Sf 1.46, when you liquidate the Swiss franc deposit of the cash-and-carry strategy. Because you want the Swiss franc deposit to yield Sf 1.46 a year from now, you must deposit the present value of Sf 1.46 at time 0, which is Sf 1.46/1.08 = Sf 1.352. At the current spot FX rate of 1.50 Sf/$, you thus need Sf 1.352/(1.50 Sf/$) = $0.9013 at time 0.

Now consider the time-1 U.S. dollar receipt on the actual forward FX contract, $1.00. You borrow the present value of $1.00 as part of the cash-and-carry strategy, knowing that the actual forward FX receipt of $1 will provide the loan repayment amount. That is, you borrow the present value of $1.00, which is $1.00/1.10 = $0.9091. Of the $0.9091 proceeds of the loan, you only need $0.9013 to do the rest of the transactions of the cash-and-carry strategy. The remainder is the arbitrage profit, $0.9091 minus $0.9013 = $0.0078. Figure 7.4 lays out the calculations.

	TODAY		IN ONE YEAR	
	Sf	US$	Sf	US$
Enter actual short forward on Swiss francs	0	0	−1.46	1.00
Borrow $1.00/1.10 = $0.9091	0	0.9091	0	−1.00
Spot FX $0.9013 to Swiss francs at 1.50 Sf/$	1.352	−0.9013	0	0
Deposit Sf1.46/1.08 = Sf 1.352	−1.352	0	1.46	0
Arbitrage profit (Today)		+0.0078		

Figure 7.4. Covered interest arbitrage cash flows.

If the actual forward FX rate instead were 1.49 Sf/$, given the synthetic forward FX rate is still 1.473 Sf/$, you would reverse the arbitrage process. In this case, you want to go long (buy) Swiss francs in an actual forward FX contract at 1.49 Sf/$ and simultaneously go short on (sell) Swiss francs at the higher synthetic forward FX price of the Swiss franc, corresponding to the synthetic forward FX rate of 1.473 Sf/$. The next example, gives the details of the trades.

Assume the actual forward FX rate is 1.49 Sf/$, and all else is the same as in the text example. You put on a covered interest arbitrage with an actual forward FX position *SIZE* of Sf 1.49. Explain the details of the arbitrage and find the arbitrage profit.

Answer: You take a long actual forward FX position on Swiss francs with contract *SIZE* of Sf 1.49 at the actual forward FX rate of 1.49 Sf/$. You figure out how much you can borrow today against your future receipt of Sf 1.49, which is Sf 1.49/1.08 = Sf 1.38. At the spot FX rate of 1.50 Sf/$, you can spot FX the Sf 1.38 into $0.9198. Next note how much you need to deliver on the actual forward FX contract, $1.00. You will be depositing the present value of $1.00, which is $1.00/1.10 = $0.9091. You can thus walk away at time 0 with the arbitrage profit of $0.9198 minus $0.9091 = $0.0107. The future cash flows of the actual long forward FX position on Swiss francs are covered by the synthetic: The proceeds of Sf 1.49 from the actual forward FX contract repays the Swiss franc loan, whereas the obliged $1.00 delivery in the actual forward is covered by money from the U.S. dollar deposit.

Summary Action Points

- A forward FX position allows you to contract today for the future receipt or payment of foreign currency at a market-determined forward FX rate.
- You receive foreign currency with a long forward FX position on foreign currency. You pay foreign currency with a short forward FX position on foreign currency.
- Synthetic forward FX contracts can be created through spot FX transactions combined with deposits and loans.
- The CIRP condition is an empirically reliable, no-arbitrage relationship between a spot FX rate, a forward FX rate, and the interest rate differential.
- Deviations from the CIRP condition are rare in the interbank market, but sometimes occur in retail user markets.
- The forward FX rate is not a good forecast of the future spot FX rate.
- Covered interest arbitrage, combining an actual FX forward position and a synthetic FX forward position, enforces the CIRP condition.

Glossary

AMOUNT (**in a forward FX contract**): The number of units of the pricing currency in a forward FX contract.

Cash-and-carry strategy: The use of currency deposits and loans to create synthetic forward FX contracts.

Covered interest rate parity (CIRP) condition: The no-arbitrage relationship between the spot FX rate, the forward FX rate, and the interest rate differential.

Covered interest arbitrage: Simultaneous transactions in the spot FX market, the forward FX market, and the interest rate market to exploit price and rate misalignments.

Difference check: A means of cash settlement on a forward FX contract that avoids physical delivery.

Forward FX contract: A contract between two parties for the future exchange of currencies at a *forward FX rate.*

Forward premium puzzle: The tendency for the FX price of a currency to rise if it has the higher interest rate, contrary to the prediction of the UIRP condition.

Long forward FX position on currency C: Receives currency C at the contract delivery date and delivers the contract's pricing currency.

Natural long (short) position in a foreign currency: A long (short) position in the foreign currency that occurs as part of normal operations.

Short forward FX position on currency C: Obligated to deliver currency C at the contract delivery date and receive the contract's pricing currency.

SIZE (in a forward FX contract): The number of units of the foreign currency in a forward FX contract.

Synthetic: An equivalent to a security that is engineered, from other existing securities.

Discussion Questions

1. Explain the advantage of the difference check settlement relative to physical delivery.
2. Explain how a synthetic long forward FX position can be constructed.
3. Compare and contrast the CIRP condition with the UIRP condition.
4. Given that the CIRP condition holds, explain why the two assertions are equivalent: (a) today's actual spot FX rate is equal to the spot FX rate that would be observed if the UIRP condition holds; (b) the forward FX rate is equal to the expected future spot FX rate, $F_N^{S/\$} = E(X_N^{S/\$})$.

Problems

1. You take a one-year short forward FX position on euros at a forward FX rate of 0.9375 \$/€. State the cash flow obligations of your short euro forward position, now and a year from now, if the contract *AMOUNT* is \$2 million. What is the contract *SIZE*?
2. You take a one-year long forward FX position on Swiss francs at a forward FX rate of 1.50 Sf/\$. State the cash flow obligations of your long forward position on Swiss francs, now and a year from now, assuming the contract *SIZE* is Sf 150 million. What is the contract *AMOUNT*?
3. You take a one-year short position in a (U.S. dollar denominated) forward FX contract on yen at a forward FX rate of $F_1^{\text{¥/\$}} = 130$ ¥/\$. The contract *AMOUNT* is \$1 million. If the spot FX rate a year from

now is $X_1^{¥/\$}$ = 120 ¥/$, what is the U.S. dollar gain (loss) on the short forward position on yen?

4. You take a long position on British pounds in a two-year (U.S. dollar denominated) forward FX contract at a forward FX rate of 1.60 $/£. The contract *AMOUNT* is $2 million. If the spot FX rate for the pound two years from now is $X_2^{\$/£}$ = 2.00 $/£, what is your gain (or loss) on the contract in U.S. dollars?

5. You take a one-year long position in a (U.S. dollar denominated) forward FX contract on yen at a forward FX rate of $F_1^{¥/\$}$ = 100 ¥/$. The contract *AMOUNT* is $1 million. If the spot FX rate for the yen a year from now is $X_1^{¥/\$}$ = 125 ¥/$, what is the U.S. dollar gain (loss) on the long forward position on yen?

6. Assume that presently the spot FX rate is 1.80 $/£ and that the actual one-year forward FX rate is 1.75 $/£. The one-year U.S. dollar interest rate is 4%; the one-year pound sterling interest rate is 5%. (a) Explain how to create a synthetic long one-year forward FX position on British pounds. (b) What is the synthetic one-year forward FX rate?

7. Assume the one-year interest rate for euros is 5% and the one-year interest rate for U.S. dollars is 3.50%. The spot FX rate is 1.25 $/€. What is the one-year forward FX rate according to the CIRP condition?

8. Assume that today the spot FX rate is 1.44 $/£. The one-year U.S. dollar interest rate is 5%; the one-year pound sterling interest rate is 7%. (a) What should be the one-year forward FX rate, if CIRP holds? (b) Assume the actual one-year forward FX rate is 1.40 $/£. Explain the arbitrage you should perform to exploit the CIRP violation in the given information and to provide you with an arbitrage profit at time 0. (c) What is the time-0 arbitrage profit for a forward FX position *AMOUNT* of $1.40 million?

9. Assume the one-year rate of interest is 7% in Canadian dollars and 5% in U.S. dollars, the actual spot FX rate is 1.25 C$/$, and the actual one-year forward FX rate is 1.26 C$/$. Determine a covered interest arbitrage strategy, and find the amount of time-0 arbitrage profits, in U.S. dollars, for an actual forward FX contract *AMOUNT* of $1,050.

10. Assume the actual one-year forward FX rate for the Japanese yen is $F_1^{¥/\$}$ = 100 ¥/$, and the actual current spot FX rate is $X_0^{¥/\$}$ = 106 ¥/$. Assume the one-year yen interest rate is $r^¥$ = 2%, and the one-year U.S. dollar interest rate is $r^\$$ = 6%. Is an arbitrage profit available? If so, show how to perform the arbitrage, and find the amount of time-0 arbitrage profit (in U.S. dollars) that can be made via covered interest arbitrage for an actual forward FX contract AMOUNT of $1,000.

Answers to Problems

1. No cash flows now; a year from now, you pay €2.133 million (the contract SIZE) and receive $2 million.

2. No cash flows now; a year from now, you receive Sf 150 million and pay $100 million (the contract AMOUNT).

3. −$83,333.

4. $500,000.

5. $Z^¥$ = ¥100 million; $D_¥^\$$ = ¥100 million(0.008 $/¥ − 0.01 $/¥) = −$200,000. The long yen position thus loses $200,000.

6. (a) Borrow U.S. dollars (issue U.S. dollar debt), buy spot pounds, and deposit the pounds. (b) (1.80 $/£)(1.04/1.05) = 1.783 $/£.

7. 1.25 $/€(1.035/1.05) = 1.232 $/€.

8. (a) (1.44 $/£)(1.05/1.07) = 1.413 $/£.

(b) The actual forward FX value of the pound (1.40 $/£) is too low compared to the theoretical forward of CIRP (1.413 $/£). Thus, take a long actual forward FX position on pounds, and a short synthetic forward FX position on pounds.

(c) For an actual FX forward contract with AMOUNT of $1.40 million, the contract SIZE = £1 million. For the synthetic short forward on pounds: first borrow £1 million/1.07 = £0.935 million, to repay £1 million next year. Convert the pounds to U.S. dollars today at the actual spot FX rate of 1.44 $/£ to get $1.346 million. You need only deposit today the PV of $1.40 million, which is $1.40 million/1.05 = $1.333 million, in order to have the necessary $1.40 million to deliver against the forward FX obligation. Your time-0 arbitrage profit is thus $1.346 million minus $1.333 million = $12,667.

9. (1.25 C\$/\$)(1.07/1.05) = 1.274 C\$/\$. The Canadian dollar has a lower synthetic forward FX price than actual. So buy C\$ forward synthetically and short C\$ forward actually. If the actual forward contract *AMOUNT* is \$1,050, the contract *SIZE* is 1.26 C\$/\$ (\$1,050) = C\$1,323. You will pay C\$1,323 and receive \$1,050 in the actual forward FX contract. So you need to deposit today C\$1,323/1.07 = C\$1,236.45. To get this amount in the spot FX market, you need C\$1,236.45/(1.25 C\$/\$) = \$989.16. You borrow \$1,050/1.05 = \$1,000. Because you only need \$989.16, your arbitrage profit = \$10.84.

10. Equation (7.3) tells us that the forward FX rate should be $(106 \ \yen/\$) \times (1.02/1.06) = 102 \ \yen/\$$. Because the actual forward FX rate is given to be 100 ¥/\$, there is an arbitrage opportunity. Because the FX price of the U.S. dollar should be 102 ¥/\$ in the forward FX market (given the other information), but is actually 100 ¥/\$, the actual forward FX price of the U.S. dollar is too low relative to the synthetic. To "buy low—sell high," the arbitrage will involve going short yen in the actual forward and going long yen in the synthetic forward. Take an actual short forward FX position on yen with $A^{\$} = \$1,000$ and thus $Z^{\yen} = \$1,000(100 \ \yen/\$) = \yen100,000$. You need to deposit ¥100,000/1.02 = ¥98,040 to cover the actual forward position's delivery obligation of ¥100,000, so you will need to buy ¥98,040 in the spot FX market at 106 ¥/\$, with ¥98,040/(106 ¥/\$) = \$925. Take a U.S. dollar loan with time-0 proceeds of \$1,000/1.06 = \$943.40, knowing you will be receiving \$1,000 from the actual forward. The arbitrage profit is \$943.40 − 925 = \$18.40.

CHAPTER 8

Foreign Exchange
Transaction Exposure

Forward foreign exchange (FX) contracts are used by many companies to help manage the risk posed by uncertain future FX rate fluctuations, called *FX transaction exposure*. This chapter covers the use of forward FX contracts in managing FX transaction exposure. This coverage includes the valuation of unsettled forward FX positions, called *mark-to-market* valuation. We also go over some basic corporate accounting implications of using forward FX contracts.

Hedging FX Transaction Exposure
with Forward FX Contracts

Although forward FX contracts can be used for speculating on the direction of FX changes, one of the important basic functions of such contracts is to *hedge*, or offset, the risk in natural FX transaction exposure. For example, assume you manage a U.S. company that has shipped products to Germany, and the terms call for payment in three months in the amount of €3 million. As we covered, your company's receivable represents a natural *long* position in euros, and the receivable has FX transaction exposure to the euro. A *short* forward FX position on euros can be used to hedge the FX transaction exposure of the natural long euro position of the receivable. For example, assume that the three-month forward FX rate is currently 1.25 $/€. A short FX forward position on euros with a contract *SIZE* of €3 million at the forward FX rate of 1.25 $/€ would obligate you to deliver €3 million and receive €3 million (1.25 $/€) = $3.75 million at the delivery time.

At the delivery time, you simply use the €3 million natural receipt to settle your forward FX contract (e.g., with your bank; banks are often forward FX counterparties as a fee-based business.) Your bank, in turn, gives you the $3.75 million at that delivery time. The receivable and the forward FX position combine for guaranteed total receipt of $3.75 million in three months' time. Although you do not receive the $3.75 million until three months later, at least you know today how many U.S. dollars you will be receiving in exchange for the €3 million you owed. Actually, a bank is usually willing to give you the discounted (present) value of the $3.75 million today.

The same outcome results if settlement is by difference check. For example, if in three months' time the spot FX rate turns out to be 1.20 $/€, the euro receivable will be worth €3 million(1.20 $/€) = $3.60 million. Using equation (7.1), a long FX forward position on euros would receive a difference check of €3 million(1.20 $/€ − 1.25 $/€) = −$150,000; this negative amount implies that your short forward position on euros would receive $150,000 in settlement from the long euro counterparty. Combining the U.S. dollar equivalent of the natural euro receipt with the difference check settlement, the net result is a receipt in U.S. dollars of $3.60 million + $150,000 = $3.75 million.

A company with a future **payable** of foreign currency, which is a natural short position on the foreign currency, may **hedge** the FX transaction exposure with a long position in a forward FX contract on the foreign currency. This idea is shown in the next example.

Assume a U.S. company is committed to making a natural payment of ¥300,000 in one year. Assume that the current one-year forward FX rate is $F_1^{¥/\$} = 120$ ¥/$.

(a) Find the U.S. dollar payout for certain when hedging with a forward FX contract.

(b) Demonstrate that, if the spot FX rate at the delivery time is $X_1^{¥/\$} = 100$ ¥/$, the difference check hedges the FX transaction exposure.

Answers: (a) At the forward FX rate of $F_1^{¥/\$} = 120$ ¥/$, the U.S. dollar value of the natural yen liability is ¥300,000/(120 ¥/$) = $2,500. Thus, $A^\$$ is $2,500, whereas $Z^¥$ is ¥300,000. So $2,500 is the U.S. dollar amount that can be locked-in in place of an exposed future natural yen payable. (b) If the spot FX rate is $X_1^{¥/\$} = 100$ ¥/$ at the delivery time, the U.S. dollar value of the yen payable will be ¥300,000/(100 ¥/$) = $3,000. If one hedges with a $2,500 long yen position in a forward FX contract, the difference check to the long yen forward position, from equation (7.1), will be ¥300,000[1/(100 ¥/$) − 1/(120 ¥/$)] = $500. The company's U.S. dollar payout, combining the U.S. dollar value of the natural yen payment ($3,000 outflow) and the gain/loss on the long forward FX position ($500 inflow), is a $2,500 net outflow.

Remember, for a natural FX receivable (a natural <u>long</u> position in a currency), you <u>hedge with a short</u> forward FX position in the currency. For a natural FX payable (a natural <u>short</u> position a currency), you <u>hedge with a long</u> forward FX position in the currency. (A long forward FX position with a receivable, or a short forward FX position with a payable, would be double exposure, and is sometimes called a "Texas hedge.")

Money Market Hedging of FX Transaction Exposure

The use of a synthetic forward FX contract (created by a cash-and-carry strategy) to hedge FX transaction exposure is sometimes referred to as a *money market hedge*. You can hedge the FX transaction exposure of a future foreign currency **receivable** by the cash-and-carry **synthetic <u>short</u>** forward FX position on the currency: (a) borrow the foreign currency; (b) spot exchange the borrowed proceeds into your home currency today; (c) deposit the home currency. Later you use the receivable cash flow to repay the borrowed foreign currency amount, and you are left with the liquidation of the base currency deposit. (Actually, you do not have to make the deposit if you want the home currency amount at time 0 rather than later.)

Similarly, you would hedge the FX transaction exposure of a future foreign currency **payable** by the cash-and-carry **synthetic <u>long</u>** forward FX position on the currency: (a) borrow the home currency; (b) spot exchange the borrowed proceeds into the foreign currency today; (c) deposit the foreign currency. Later you use the liquidation of the foreign currency deposit to make the payable, and you repay the home currency loan.

The disadvantage of money market hedging is that the practice tends to inflate corporate balance sheets. That is, a deposit must be shown on the financial statements as an asset, and a loan must be shown as a liability. Although the two items initially offset each other in value, their mere presence on the balance sheet will alter the financial ratios that external analysts calculate to assess a company's creditworthiness. An actual forward FX contract serves the same purpose as a money market hedge, but is an "off-balance sheet" position. There are some balance sheet implications for forward FX positions that we will cover shortly, but these are of a much smaller magnitude than for the money market hedge.

Figure 8.1 shows a comparison of the initial balance sheet implications of the two ways of hedging a natural long FX transaction exposure: (a) a money market hedge, which goes on the balance sheet, and (b) an equivalent forward FX position, which is "off-balance sheet." We assume that the company takes a two-year short forward FX position on euros. The time-0 spot FX rate is 1.25 $/€, the annualized two-year interest rate is 4% in U.S. dollars and 6% in euros. So, by the covered interest rate parity (CIRP) condition, the two-year forward FX rate is $1.25 \ \$/€(1.04/1.06)^2 = 1.2264 \ \$/€$. The contract's SIZE $(Z^€)$ is €898.88 and AMOUNT $(A^\$)$ is $1,081.60.

Money market hedge vs forward FX contract		
A. Money market hedge—short euros		
Assets	_Debt and equity_	
$1,000 USD Deposit	$1,000 Loan (€800; Face = €898.88)	
$2,000 Rest of assets	$2,000 Rest of debt and equity	
$3,000 Total	$3,000 Total	
B. Actual forward FX position—short euros		
Assets	_Debt and equity_	
(Off) $1,000 $PV^\$(A^\$)$ $A^\$ = \$1081.60$	$1,000 $PV^\$(Z^€)$ (≡ €800) $Z^€ = €898.88$	
$2,000 Assets	$2,000 Debt and equity	
$2,000 Total	$2,000 Total	

Figure 8.1. Initial balance sheet implications.

For the money market hedge (Figure 8.1A), the firm borrows euros with a face value of €898.88 for two years, for proceeds of €898.88/1.06^2 = €800, which is equivalent to $1,000. So the euro loan goes on the firm's balance sheet as a $1,000 liability. The loan proceeds are converted to U.S. dollars, and then deposited for two years (at 4%), which is shown as an asset. The equivalent actual short forward FX position is "off-balance sheet" and is thus shown above the dotted line in Panel B. Panel B shows the present value (PV) of the forward FX contract's *SIZE* (in U.S. dollars) on the right-hand side as an implicit, off-balance sheet liability, and the PV of the forward FX contract's *AMOUNT* on the left-hand side as an implicit, off-balance sheet asset.

If the CIRP condition holds, implying that the actual forward FX rate is equal to the synthetic forward FX rate implicit in the money market hedge, why use a money market hedge instead of an actual forward FX position? The answer is that the CIRP condition tends to hold only in the interbank FX market where currency traders interact. Instead, the typical hedger faces retail interest rates and retail forward FX rates that include a mark-up by the hedger's bank. Many times, the actual retail FX forward rate will be a better for the corporate hedger than the synthetic retail forward FX rate, even if the CIRP condition holds with interbank rates. But other times, the synthetic retail forward FX rate is better than the actual retail forward FX rate; so the hedger would prefer a money market hedge. However, there are two qualitative considerations as well. First, as we said, the money market hedge has the balance sheet implications that an actual forward FX position does not. Second, some companies do not like the idea of using derivatives at all, even for hedging. Such companies might prefer the money market hedge approach even if the numbers are worse. The box on Baker Adhesives has additional discussion.

Baker Adhesives

There is a Darden School (University of Virginia) case on hedging FX transaction exposure, titled Baker Adhesives.[1] The case is set in 2006, when New Jersey-based Baker Adhesives Co. (a real company, now named Baker-Titan Adhesives) had developed a customer that was a

Brazilian toy maker named Novo. Novo insisted on pricing in its home currency, the Brazilian real, and Baker agreed. The case explains that when Novo paid the invoice for its first shipment from Baker, the Brazilian real had depreciated substantially from the time of the pricing agreement between the two companies. So in U.S. dollars, Baker's revenues from the transaction were much smaller than had been anticipated.

From this experience, Baker is considering hedging the FX transaction exposure on a second shipment. The case gives information on the retail spot and forward FX rates available to Baker, and then asks two basic questions. For one question, we are given a forecasted spot FX price of the Brazilian real that is higher than the forward FX price. The question is whether Baker should hedge or not, because it is tempting for Baker to consider not hedging. Of course, there is really no correct answer to this question. The question is designed to make the student think about the risk borne when the hedging is not done.

For the other question, the case supplies a retail borrowing rate in Brazilian real that was available to Baker, as well as the available retail deposit rate in U.S. dollars. The question is whether the actual forward FX contract is better than the money market hedging approach. Of course, there _is_ a correct quantitative answer to this question, which depends on the numbers. In addition, the qualitative considerations in the decision are the balance sheet implications for the money market hedge versus the "stigma" of using derivatives that some companies try to avoid.

A U.S. importer has a euro payable due in one year. The spot FX rate is 1.30 $/€ today. Today, the importer's bank quotes an actual retail one-year forward FX rate of 1.28 $/€. At time 0 (now), the importer can deposit euros at 5%, and can borrow U.S. dollars at 3%. At time 0, the importer decides to hedge the FX transaction exposure of the euro payable with a money market hedge.

(A) What are the transactions of this hedge?

(B) What is the synthetic forward FX rate?

(C) Ignoring qualitative implications and any possible transaction costs, which alternative is better: (a) hedge the payable's FX exposure with an actual forward FX contract; (b) hedge the payable's FX exposure with the money market hedge; or (c) neither (a) nor (b)?

Answers: (A) To hedge a euro payable, you go long euros in the synthetic forward position: Borrow U.S. dollars for one year, spot FX the proceeds of the loan into euros, deposit the euros for a year; (B) (1.30 \$/€)(1.03/1.05) = 1.275 \$/€; (C) (b) Because you hedge the euro payable with a long forward FX position on euros, it is cheaper to buy euros forward with the synthetic forward (1.275 \$/€) than with the actual (1.28 \$/€).

Mark-to-Market Value of a Forward FX Contract

As forward FX rates in the market change, given a contract's set forward FX rate, the contract's market value fluctuates and may be positive or negative. The market value of an unsettled forward FX contract position is called the *mark-to-market (MTM) value*. The MTM value of any financial position is the PV of the future inflows minus the PV of the future outflows. To mean anything, this valuation must be consistently expressed in one specific currency. When the components are in different currencies, as is the case in a forward FX contract, the PV of each component is first found in its own currency, using market interest rates (yields) applicable to that currency. Then the current spot FX rate can be used to convert the PVs into the MTM value expressed in one currency. Letting $M^\$$ represent MTM value in U.S. dollars, the idea is shown in equation (8.1a).

Mark-To-Market Value

$$M^\$ = PV^\$ \, (Receipts) - PV^\$ \, (Payments) \qquad (8.1a)$$

The MTM value of a forward FX contract on Swiss francs can be found by netting the PVs of the forward contract's future cash flows, using the current spot FX rate to combine the two PV components into a common currency. A (U.S. dollar denominated) long forward position on Swiss francs is equivalent to owning a Swiss franc receipt and owing a U.S. dollar payment. The Swiss franc receipt is the forward contract's *SIZE*, Z^{Sf}, and the U.S. dollar payment is the contract's *AMOUNT*, $A^{\$}$.

Note that if the FX forward rate is correctly aligned with the CIRP condition, a forward FX contract's MTM value is 0 when the contract originates. That is, the PV of the contract *SIZE* and *AMOUNT* are equal, given the spot FX rate. For example, assume a spot FX rate of 1.10 Sf/$, and one-year interest rates of 5% in Swiss francs and 10% in U.S. dollars. So the one-year forward FX rate is 1.10 Sf/$(1.05/1.10) = 1.05 Sf/$, given that the CIRP condition holds. Consider the long Swiss franc position for *SIZE* of Z^{Sf} = Sf 105,000, so the contract's *AMOUNT* is $A^{\$}$ = $100,000. The PV of the Sf 105,000 receipt is Sf 105,000/1.05 = Sf 100,000, which at the spot FX rate of 1.10 Sf/$ is equivalent to Sf 100,000/(1.10 Sf/$) = $90,909 in U.S. dollars. The PV of the $100,000 owed is $100,000/1.10 = $90,909. Using equation (8.1a), the MTM value in U.S. dollars at the contract's origination, the PV in U.S. dollars of the receipts ($90,909) minus the PV in U.S. dollars of the payments ($90,909), is 0.

After a forward FX contract's origination, the MTM value fluctuates as the market conditions change for the spot FX rate and the interest rates in the two currencies. For example, suppose three months (1/4 year) have elapsed since the one-year forward FX contract was established at the forward FX rate of 1.05 Sf/$. Again assume the contract *AMOUNT* of $A^{\$}$ = $100,000 and thus a contract *SIZE* of Z^{Sf} = Sf 105,000. Assume that now the annualized nine-month interest rate is 6% in Swiss francs and 9% in U.S. dollars. Assume further that the spot FX rate at this time is 1.08 Sf/$. The PV of the Sf 105,000 receipt is Sf 105,000/$1.06^{0.75}$ = Sf 100,510, which at the spot FX rate of 1.08 Sf/$ is equivalent to Sf 100,510/ (1.08 Sf/$) = $93,065 in U.S. dollars. The PV of the $100,000 owed is $100,000/$1.09^{0.75}$ = $93,741. So in U.S. dollars, the MTM value of the long forward FX position on Swiss francs is equal to $93,065 − 93,741 = −$676.

Another way to view the MTM value is with the nine-month FX forward rate. If the CIRP condition holds, the nine-month FX forward rate at the time we calculate the MTM value is (1.08 Sf/$)(1.06/1.09)$^{0.75}$ = 1.0576 Sf/$. A trader holding a long forward position on Sf 105,000 could "unwind" the position by selling Sf 105,000 nine-months forward at 1.0576 Sf/$, contracting to receive Sf 105,000/(1.0576 Sf/$) = $99,279. Because the original position's payment was to have been $100,000 at that time, you see that there is now a built-in loss of $99,279 − 100,000 = −$721 nine months from now. When we take the PV of that loss, we get −$721/1.09$^{0.75}$ = −$676. It is no accident that this MTM value is exactly equal to the one we first computed.

The negative MTM value in this case represents an amount that the long forward position on Swiss francs would have to pay to liquidate the position to someone else in the market, given that the spot FX rate is 1.08 Sf/$. The MTM value of the long position on Swiss francs is negative mainly because at 1.08 Sf/$, the spot FX price of the Swiss franc is lower than at the contract's forward FX rate of 1.05 Sf/$. Also, changes in interest rates since the forward contract originated will have an influence on a forward FX contract's MTM value.

A *short* forward position on Swiss francs, with contract *SIZE* equal to Sf 105,000, pays Sf 105,000 and receives $100,000 nine months from now, and thus has a positive MTM value today, of $93,741 − 93,065 = $676. This MTM value represents what the short forward position on Swiss francs would receive through unwinding and liquidating the position in the market. The short forward position on Swiss francs benefits from the low spot FX price of the Swiss franc (1.08 Sf/$), relative to the contract's forward FX rate (1.05 Sf/$).

In general, the MTM value of a *long* forward position on Swiss francs, in U.S. dollars, is equal to the PV of the Swiss franc receipt, adjusted into U.S. dollars at the current spot FX rate, minus the PV of the U.S. dollar payment. This value is given by equation (8.1*b*), where *n* represents the number of years left until the delivery time of the forward FX contract that had *N* years until delivery when it originated.

MTM Value of Forward FX Position
Long Swiss Francs

$$M_{Sf}^{\$} = X_0^{\$/Sf}[Z^{Sf}/(1 + r^{Sf})^n] - A^{\$}/(1 + r^{\$})^n \qquad (8.1b)$$

As usual, the *super*script symbol denotes the currency in which a security or contract is denominated, whereas the *sub*script symbol denotes the exposure currency. So in $M_{Sf}^\$$, the U.S. dollar is the pricing currency for the forward FX contract and the MTM value is exposed to changes in (the FX price of) the Swiss franc. The MTM value of a long forward FX position on Swiss francs, $M_{Sf}^\$$, is priced in U.S. dollars. The first term on the right-hand side of equation (8.1*b*) is the PV of the contract's Swiss franc receipt, adjusted into U.S. dollars at the current spot FX rate, and the term after the minus sign is the PV of the contract's U.S. dollar payment.

For example, consider again the forward FX contract that originated as a one-year contract at the forward FX rate of 1.05 Sf/$. Recall the assumptions that three months after origination the spot FX rate is 1.08 Sf/$, the annualized nine-month market interest rates are 6% in Swiss francs and 9% in U.S. dollars. First, reciprocate the current spot FX rate of 1.08 Sf/$ into direct terms from the U.S. point of view, to get 1/(1.08 Sf/$) = 0.9259 $/Sf. Then equation (8.1*b*) says that the MTM value of the long position on Swiss francs, with Z^{Sf} = Sf 105,000 and thus $A^\$$ = $100,000, should be (0.9259 $/Sf) (Sf 105,000/1.06$^{0.75}$) – $100,000/1.09$^{0.75}$ = –$676. The MTM value of the short position is just the negative of the MTM value to the long position. The MTM value of the short position on Swiss francs = $676.

A year ago a U.S. firm took a two-year long forward FX position on euros with a contract *AMOUNT* of $A^\$$ = $100. Assume that the two-year forward FX rate was $F_2^{\$/€}$ = 1.164 $/€. Thus the contract *SIZE* is $Z^€$ = $100/(1.164 $/€) = €85.91. At the present time, with a year left until the delivery time, assume that the spot FX rate is 1.05 $/€, the one-year U.S. dollar interest rate is 6.20%, and the one-year euro interest rate is 3.60%. What is the MTM value now of the long forward FX position taken a year ago?

Answer: Using equation (8.1*b*), the MTM value of the long forward FX position on euros is equal to (1.05 $/€)(€85.91/1.036) – $100/ 1.062 = –$7.09.

Accounting for Forward FX Contracts

Accounting rules require that the MTM value of an unsettled forward FX position must be included on the company's balance sheet. A positive

MTM value is an asset; a negative MTM value is a liability. The European aircraft manufacturer Airbus, for example, has both short-term and long-term liability accounts for cumulative negative MTM values, depending on the term of the contract. (See the box on Airbus for more details.) However, companies that hedge only short-term cash flows sometimes net the cumulative MTM values on the various instruments into the more general asset account "cash and marketable securities."

In addition, if the forward FX contract is not a hedge, possibly because it is a speculative position, the MTM change in each reporting period must be included in the computation of that period's current earnings. For example, consider the previous example where the long forward position on euros has an MTM value of −$7.09. Given that the forward FX position had an MTM value of 0 initially, the change in the position's MTM value is −$7.09. Accounting rules require that this loss be reflected in the corporate earnings for the current year, although the company's forward FX position is still "alive." This loss will affect retained earnings and thus accumulated retained earnings in the equity section of the balance sheet.

However, if a forward FX position is a hedge of an FX transaction exposure, the hedging company may be able to elect *hedge accounting* treatment for the position's MTM changes, where the MTM change each reporting period avoids being considered as earnings until the cash flow being hedged becomes earnings. Instead, the MTM change is reflected in the company's other comprehensive income, and is "parked" in the balance sheet equity account known as *accumulated other comprehensive income (AOCI)*.

To qualify as a hedge of an anticipated cash flow under SFAS 133, a hedge position must pass a test for *hedge effectiveness*. The firm must file written documentation, before taking a hedge position, if it wants the position to qualify as a cash flow hedge. This formal documentation must include: (a) identification of the hedging instrument and the hedged item or transaction; (b) the nature of the risk being hedged, including proof of a high probability that the cash flow will occur; (c) the risk management objective or strategy; and (d) how hedging effectiveness will be assessed. Hedge effectiveness must be reviewed frequently; if a hedge position no longer passes the test, changes in the MTM value of the position must be immediately and fully recorded in current earnings. A complication is that a hedge position might only partially hedge some underlying risk. In this case, the hedge-ineffective portion must be measured and included in current reported earnings. This accounting treatment is part of both U.S. GAAP and international accounting standards. The Altria Group box also has a discussion of these issues.

Altria Group

Note 17 to 2002 Consolidated Financial Statements

Altria Group, Inc. operates globally, with manufacturing and sales facilities in various locations around the world, and utilizes certain financial instruments to manage its foreign currency and commodity exposures, which primarily relate to forecasted transactions and debt. Derivative financial instruments are used by Altria Group, Inc., principally to reduce exposures to market risks resulting from fluctuations in FX rates and commodity prices, by creating offsetting exposures. Altria Group, Inc. is not a party to leveraged derivatives and, by policy, does not use derivative financial instruments for speculative purposes. Financial instruments qualifying for hedge accounting must maintain a specified level of effectiveness between the hedging instrument and the item being hedged, both at inception and throughout the hedged period. Altria Group, Inc. formally documents the nature and relationships between the hedging instruments and hedged items, as well as its risk-management objectives, strategies for undertaking the various hedge transactions and method of assessing hedge effectiveness. Additionally, for hedges of forecasted transactions, the significant characteristics and expected terms of a forecasted transaction must be specifically identified, and it must be probable that each forecasted transaction will occur. If it were deemed probable that the forecasted transaction will not occur, the gain or loss would be recognized in earnings currently.

A substantial portion of Altria Group, Inc.'s derivative financial instruments is effective as hedges under SFAS No. 133. Altria Group, Inc. uses forward FX contracts and foreign currency options to mitigate its exposure to changes in exchange rates from third-party and intercompany forecasted transactions. The primary currencies to which Altria Group, Inc. is exposed include the Japanese yen, Swiss franc, and the euro. At December 31, 2002 and 2001, Altria Group, Inc. had option and forward FX contracts with aggregate notional amounts of $10.1 billion and $3.7 billion, respectively, which are comprised of contracts for the purchase and sale of foreign currencies. Included in the foreign currency aggregate notional amounts at December 31, 2002, were $2.6 billion of equal and offsetting foreign currency positions, which do not qualify as hedges and that will not result in any net gain or loss. The effective portion of unrealized gains and losses associated with forward contracts and the value of option contracts is deferred as a component of accumulated other comprehensive losses until the underlying hedged transactions are reported on Altria Group, Inc.'s consolidated statement of earnings.

The balance sheet implications of the MTM accounting for an actual short forward FX position on euros are shown in Figure 8.2. The initial position is the same as the scenario for Figure 8.1. The time-0 spot FX rate is 1.25 $/€, the annualized two-year interest rate is 4% in U.S. dollars and 6% in euros. The two-year forward FX rate is 1.25 $/€$(1.04/1.06)^2$ = 1.2264 $/€. The contract's *SIZE* €898.88 and *AMOUNT* is $1,081.60. We assume that a year later (time 1) the spot FX rate is 1.30 $/€, and the one-year interest rates are 4% in U.S. dollars and 6% in euros. Using equation (8.1b), the MTM value of the forward FX position is $1081.60/1.04 − (1.30 $/€)(€898.88/1.06) = $1,040 − 1,102.40 = −$62.40. In Figure 8.2, this MTM loss is shown as a negative amount on the asset side (a "contra asset") of the time-1 balance sheet.

If the forward FX position does NOT qualify for hedge accounting treatment, the MTM change IS part of the company's current earnings for the year ending at time 1, and the time-1 balance sheet impact shows in accumulated retained earnings (see Figure 8.2B). If the forward FX position DOES qualify for hedge accounting treatment, the MTM change is NOT part of the company's current earnings for the year ending at time 1, and the time-1 balance sheet impact shows in AOCI (see Figure 8.2C).

A. Time 0:	Assets	Debt and equity
(Off)	$1,000 $PV^\$(A\$)^\$$	$1,000 $PV^\$(Z^{€})$ ($\equiv$ €800)
	$A^\$ = \$1,081.60$	$Z^{€} = €898.88$

		500 Acc ret earnings
		500 AOCI
		1,000 Common stock
	$2,000 Assets	$2,000 Total equity
	$2,000 Total	$2,000 Total

B. Time 1: No hedge accounting

	Assets	Debt and equity
(Off)	$1,040 $PV^\$(A\$)^\$$	$1,102.40 $PV^\$(Z^{€})$ ($\equiv$ €848)
	$A^\$ = \$1,081.60$	$Z^{€} = €898.88$

	−$ 62.40 Unrealized MTM	437.60 Acc ret earnings
		500 AOCI
		1,000 Common stock
	$2,000 Other assets	$1,937.60 Total equity
	$1,937.60 Total	$1,937.60 Total

C. Time 1: Hedge accounting

	Assets	Debt and equity
(Off)	$1,040 $PV^\$(A\$)^\$$	$1,102.40 $PV^\$(Z^{€})$ ($\equiv$ €848)
	$A^\$ = \$1,081.60$	$Z^{€} = €898.88$

	−$62.40 Unrealized MTM	500 Acc ret earnings
		437.60 AOCI
		1,000 Common stock
	$2,000 Other assets	$1,937.60 Total equity
	$1,937.60 Total	$1,937.60 Total

Figure 8.2. Accounting for actual forward FX contract.

Airbus

The giant European aircraft manufacturer, Airbus, prices its commercial aircraft in the standard currency of the industry, U.S. dollars. At any point in time, Airbus has contracts to deliver aircraft, and receive U.S. dollar revenues, for up to 10 years in the future, or longer. Because the company receives its revenues in U.S. dollars, but much of the operating costs are in euros, Airbus would be severely and adversely affected by a lower future FX price of the U.S. dollar (in terms of euros).

Airbus has stated that it fully hedges its revenues for two years out, and partially hedges the revenues for three to six years out, against a drop in the FX price of the U.S. dollar. For purposes of FX hedging, Airbus uses short positions on the U.S. dollar in long-dated forward FX contracts. (Airbus also uses some currency swaps and FX option contracts, which are covered elsewhere.)

Accounting rules allow a company to choose between two methods to compute MTM value: (a) use a formula like equation (8.1b); or (b) use an actual observed forward FX rate for a time to delivery equal to the time left on the forward FX position. In theory, as explained in the text, these two methods will give the same answer if the CIRP condition holds. But in reality, minor deviations from the CIRP condition may influence the choice of method. Indeed, Airbus's Dutch-listed parent, European Aeronautic Defence and Space Company, disclosed on p. 15 of its 2011 Annual Report that it changed methods because of the "dissolving of no-arbitrage relations."

Note that the hedge accounting rules also apply for a money market hedge as for an actual forward FX contract. Under "fair value accounting" for the deposit and loan, the net impact on earnings and the book value of equity are the same as with an actual forward FX contract. The scenario is shown in Figure 8.3.

Today, the spot FX rate is 1 $/€. For any maturity, the interest rate is 4% in U.S. dollars and is 6% in euros. So, by the CIRP condition, today's two-year forward FX rate is equal to 1 $/€(1.04/1.06)^2 = 0.9626 $/€. A U.S. company considers an actual two-year forward FX position to sell 1 euro for $0.9626. Alternatively, the company considers an equivalent synthetic two-year short forward position on euros: borrowing euros on a two-year discount loan with face value of €1, and time-0 proceeds of €1/1.06^2 = €0.89, converting the proceeds to U.S. dollars at the spot FX rate (1 $/€) to get $0.89, and then depositing at 4% for two years to liquidate then at $0.89(1.04^2) = $0.9626. Assume one year elapses, interest rates are unchanged, and the new spot FX rate is $1.20 $/€.

A. Time 0:

Assets		Debt and equity	
$1,000 USD Deposit		$1,000 Loan (€800) (Face: €898.88)	
		500	Acc ret earnings
		500	AOCI
		1,000	Common stock
$2,000	Other assets	$2,000	Total equity
$3,000	Total	$3,000	Total

B. Time 1: No hedge accounting

Assets		Debt and equity	
$1,040 USD Deposit		$1,102.40 Loan (€848) (Face: €898.88)	
		437.60	Acc ret earnings
		500	AOCI
		1,000	Common stock
$2,000	Other assets	$1,937.60	Total equity
$3,040	Total	$3,040	Total

C. Time 1: Hedge accounting

Assets		Debt and equity	
$1,040 USD Deposit		$1,102.40 Loan (€848) (Face: €898.88)	
		500	Acc ret earnings
		437.60	AOCI
		1,000	Common stock
$2,000	Other assets	$1,937.60	Total equity
$3,040	Total	$3,040	Total

Figure 8.3. Accounting for money market hedge.

(a) Find the MTM value of the actual forward FX position after the year elapses;

(b) Find the MTM value of the synthetic forward FX position after the year elapses.

(c) If the company is NOT hedging, what is the accounting treatment for the MTM change in each of the cases (actual and synthetic)?

(d) If the company is hedging, what is the accounting treatment for the MTM change in each of the cases (actual and synthetic)?

Answers:

(a) The actual forward FX position's MTM value is $0.9626/1.04 – (€1/1.06)(1.20 $/€) = –$0.2065. This is also the change in the position's MTM value, because the initial MTM value was 0.

(b) After one year, the value of the U.S. dollar deposit is $0.89(1.04) = $0.9256, whereas the new value of the euro loan is €1/1.06 = €0.9434. Given the new spot FX rate of 1.20 $/€, the net value of the synthetic position is $0.9256 − €0.9434(1.20 $/€) = −$0.2065.

(c) Regardless of whether the company is hedging or not, the MTM change is reflected on the balance sheet. If the company is not hedging, the MTM change must be reflected in current earnings, regardless of whether the position is actual or synthetic. The accumulated retained earnings account in the equity section will reflect the MTM gain/loss.

(d) If the company is hedging, and has documented the hedge, the company may elect hedge accounting treatment for the MTM change, regardless of whether the hedge position is actual or synthetic. The MTM change is NOT reflected in current earnings, regardless of whether the position is actual or synthetic. The accumulated other comprehensive earnings account (AOCI) in the equity section will reflect the MTM gain/loss.

To Hedge or Not?

If the spot FX rate is correctly valued, or if managers think they should not take a view on the future FX rate direction, the decision to hedge seems like an obvious winner in terms of reducing risk. However, there may be a bit more to this issue, as the box on Peugeot–Citroen suggests. In that scenario, a manager regretted hedging after the fact, because he missed out on windfall FX gains that would have been had if not for the hedging.

A similar issue related to the hedging decision arises if managers do want to take a view on the future direction of an FX rate. Sometimes managers will hedge if they think the FX rate will change in the direction that would imply a loss, but not if they forecast an FX rate change in the direction that would imply a profit. This speculative practice is called *selective hedging*. In Chapter 5, we mentioned that in February 2004, the average one-year bank forecast was 1.32 $/€, whereas the actual one-year forward FX rate was 1.245 $/€. Put yourself in the shoes of a U.S. exporter with a euro receivable due in a year's time. What would you have done:

(a) hedge the receivable using the forward FX contract, locking in 1.245 $/€; or (b) not hedge in the hopes that the bankers have some ability to forecast?[2]

The February 2004 scenario is a case where the euro was undervalued at its actual spot FX rate relative to the short-run financial market intrinsic FX rate. Some managers with a euro receivable might think this situation is a good time to not hedge, or to only partially hedge the exposed receivable. Of course, the extent of FX misvaluation would drive the extent of the hedging. As there is no formula to guide this decision at present, managers would have to use their judgment. The downside of a decision to not fully hedge the receivable is that the manager must live with the risk that the euro could drop over the next year, even though the euro is deemed to be undervalued at time 0.

Consider the opposite scenario in which the company has a euro receivable and the euro is overvalued at time 0. In this case, it seems like a "no-brainer" to hedge the euro receivable with a short FX forward position on euros. In fact, a manager might even consider "overhedging," by taking a forward FX position that is larger than the exposed receivable. This speculative decision will be profitable if the euro drops from its overvalued rate, but here there are two downsides: (a) the euro might instead rise over the next year despite being overvalued at time 0; and (b) there will be accounting implications of the excess portion of the forward FX position that would not qualify for hedge accounting.

Peugeot–Citroen

Many companies hedge FX exposure and many do not. When the euro appreciated unilaterally in 2003, European multinationals that did not hedge experienced lower profits in euros from foreign currency revenues. In the auto sector, most European carmakers successfully hedged their overseas revenue against a rising euro. One company that did not hedge was the French carmaker, Peugeot–Citroen. The appreciation of the euro wiped out €600 million of Peugeot's profit.

Peugeot's Chief Financial Officer gave the reason that hedging was like gambling. Because hedging locks in a future foreign currency cash flow at a known FX rate, if the foreign currency depreciates, the hedging strategy wins in that the losses are covered, but if the foreign currency appreciates, the hedging strategy loses in that the windfall profits are foregone. In 2003, many European carmakers won and Peugeot lost. But the CFO argued that no one could predict short-term FX movements. Had the euro depreciated, Peugeot would have won and the others would have lost.

One problem with the hedging strategy is that forward FX contracts are often not well understood by the general public. Thus, if a company hedges and foregoes a windfall FX profit, the company's investors may be upset that about the use of the hedging strategy. This is exactly what happened to Peugeot's CFO in 1997; he hedged to protect Peugeot's U.K. sales against a decline in the FX price of the pound relative to the euro. Investors focused only on the FX losses on the forward FX hedge positions and were shocked.

The lesson learned by the CFO in 1997 was that investors tend to dislike more severely lost opportunities for a windfall gain than losses due to lack of hedging. That is, investors have a psychological bias of being less concerned about losses than missing out on what might have been.

Source: "Peugeot Won't Budge as Euro Gains Strength," Wall Street Journal, November 11, 2003.

You can also think of these issues in a euro payable scenario, where hedging would require a long forward FX position. If the euro is overvalued at time 0, the firm may not want to fully hedge, trading-off the anticipated FX gain on the unhedged portion of the payable with the risk that the euro could appreciate even though it is overvalued. If the euro is undervalued at time 0, the firm may want to overhedge, trading-off the anticipated FX gain on the excess portion of the long forward FX position with (a) the risk that the euro could depreciate even though it is undervalued, and (b) the accounting implications of the excess portion of the forward FX position that would not qualify for hedge accounting.

Some managers who want to include their FX forecast "view" in the hedging decision will take positions in FX options, like puts and calls on foreign currencies. Options are a way to limit downside losses, but not windfall gains, but a fee must be paid for this approach. Further discussion in beyond this text, but readers can easily find information about FX options via a web search.

FX Futures

In basic concept, an *FX futures contract* is both like and unlike a forward FX contract. Like a forward contract, a futures contract is an obligation by two parties to exchange currencies at a set delivery time at a contract-specified FX rate. Unlike forward FX contracts, which are the instruments of the vast over-the-counter currency market, FX futures contracts are traded on particular exchanges in the world. To be traded on an exchange requires that contracts be standardized for ease of secondary market liquidation. For this reason, FX futures contracts have standardized delivery *dates*, rather than the standardized maturities of FX forward contracts. For example, a three-month forward FX contract may be originated at any time in the FX market for settlement in three months, but FX futures contracts that are available offer delivery on only certain days of certain months. Another difference is that the MTM value of a futures contract is cash-settled every day, as the market-determined futures FX rate fluctuates.

Because forwards and futures are similar, financial arbitrage between exchange-traded FX futures contracts and interbank forward FX contracts should keep FX futures contract rates near forward FX rates for the same horizon. Actually, volatile daily interest rates and the MTM feature may cause FX futures rates to differ slightly from forward FX rates. FX futures trading accounts for such a small portion of FX contract trading that we concentrate on forwards and do not differentiate the two. Technically, the text deals with forward FX contracts, but you could substitute "futures" for "forwards," and the general mechanics and valuation methods would still apply to a close approximation.

Summary Action Points

- Companies use forward FX contracts to hedge FX transaction exposure of foreign currency receivables and payables.
- A money market hedge is economically equivalent to a forward FX hedge, but the former is "on balance sheet," whereas the latter is "off-balance sheet."
- Retail corporate users of forward FX contracts may sometimes find that money market hedging with synthetic forward FX positions is

advantageous over hedging with actual forward FX positions, if the balance sheet consequences are tolerable.

- A forward FX position has a market-determined MTM value between the position's origination and delivery time. The MTM value is the PV of the future receipts minus the PV of the future payments, viewed in a common currency.

- The accounting treatment of the MTM gains and losses on a forward FX position depends on whether or not the position is hedging FX transaction exposure.

Glossary

Accumulated other comprehensive income (AOCI): An equity account used to reserve valuation changes that are not considered to be current earnings.

FX futures contract: Essentially the same as a forward contract, but with some distinctions, especially the feature of daily settlement, referred to as MTM.

Foreign exchange (FX) transaction exposure: The uncertainty in the home currency value of a contracted foreign currency amount.

Hedging: The use of a financial instrument to reduce or eliminate uncertainty about future cash flows or asset values.

Mark-to-market (MTM) value: The market value of a position that has not been liquidated and with time remaining until maturity.

Money market hedge: The use of currency deposits and loans in a cash-and-carry strategy to create synthetic forward FX contracts to hedge FX exposure.

Natural long (short) position in a foreign currency: A long (short) position in the foreign currency that occurs as part of normal operations.

Other comprehensive income (OCI): An income account reflecting valuation changes that are not considered to be current earnings.

Selective hedging: The practice of hedging FX exposure when the FX price is forecasted to change in the direction that would imply a loss, but not if the forecast is in the direction that would imply a profit.

Discussion Questions

1. Explain why a company might want to take a long position on a foreign currency in a forward FX contract.

2. Explain why a company might want to take a long position on a foreign currency in a forward FX contract.

3. Explain the issues for a retail corporate hedger of an actual forward FX position versus a money market hedge.

4. Explain the difference in the accounting treatment of a forward FX position's MTM changes if the position is hedging FX transaction exposure versus if the position is speculative.

Problems

1. A U.S. importer has a euro payable due in one year. Today, the spot FX rate is 1.40 $/€ and the one-year forward FX rate is 1.35 $/€. At time 0, the importer decides to hedge the FX transaction exposure of the euro payable with a forward FX contract with an *AMOUNT* equal to $100,000. The spot FX rate a year from now turns out to be 1.30 $/€. (a) If the importer's forward FX position is settled by a difference check a year later at the delivery time, how much is the difference check, and does the importer pay or receive? (b) In retrospect at time 1, does the importer regret that he hedged or not? Explain.

2. A U.S. importer has a euro payable due in one year. At time 0, the importer decides to hedge the FX transaction exposure of the euro payable with a money market hedge ("cash-and-carry strategy" to create a synthetic forward FX position.) What are the transactions of this hedge?

3. Today, the spot FX rate is 1.40 $/€ and the actual one-year forward FX rate is 1.35 $/€. The importer in the previous problem can deposit euros for one year at an interest rate of 6%, and can borrow U.S. dollars for one year at an interest rate of 4%. Ignoring balance sheet implications and transaction costs, which alternative is better: (a) hedge the payable's FX exposure with the actual forward FX contract; (b) hedge the payable's FX exposure with the money market hedge; or (c) neither (a) nor (b)? Explain.

4. XYZ Co. established a long two-year forward FX contract on yen a year ago at a forward FX rate of 112 ¥/$. The contract's *AMOUNT* is $1 million and the delivery time is a year from now. The current spot FX rate is 102 ¥/$. The one-year U.S. dollar interest rate is currently 6.50% and the one-year yen interest rate is currently 2%. What is the MTM value in U.S. dollars of the long forward position on yen?

5. ABC Co. established a short two-year forward FX position on yen a year ago at a forward FX rate of 125 ¥/$. The contract's *AMOUNT* is $1 million and the delivery time is a year from now. The current spot FX rate is 112 ¥/$. The one-year U.S. dollar interest rate is currently 5% and the one-year yen interest rate is currently 1%. What is the MTM value in U.S. dollars of the short forward position on yen?

6. Assume ABC Co. took the forward FX position in the previous problem to hedge a predictable yen cash inflow of ¥125 million due two years later. Assume that after one year, ABC still holds the forward FX position. (a) How does the MTM value of the position affect current earnings and book equity? (b) What if the forward FX position is not a hedge?

Answers to Problems

1. (a) The forward FX contract *SIZE* = $100,000/(1.35 $/€) = €74,000 (rounded). The difference check to the long forward FX position is €74,000(1.30 $/€ − 1.35 $/€) = −$3,700. The importer pays the check because he takes a long forward FX position on euros as a hedge of a euro payable.

   (b) Regret. The actual spot FX rate at time 1 turned out to be a lower FX price of the euro than the one-year forward FX price of the euro at time 0.

2. Borrow U.S. dollars for a year, spot FX the proceeds into euros at time 0, and deposit the euros for a year.

3. The synthetic forward FX rate equals 1.40 $/€ (1.04/1.06) = 1.37 $/€. It would be cheaper to buy euros for 1.35 $/€ with the actual forward FX contract than via the synthetic route at 1.37 $/€.

4. The long forward position on yen would have an MTM value of (¥112 million/1.02)/(102 ¥/$) − $1 million/1.065 = $0.1375 million, that is, $137,500.

5. The long forward position on yen would have an MTM value of (¥125 million/1.01)/(112 ¥/$) − $1 million/1.05 = $152,640. Because you are short, the position's MTM value is −$152,640.

6. (a) The MTM change from 0 to −$152,640 is an unrealized loss that is not included in current earnings because the position is a hedge of a predictable cash flow. But the loss results in a reduction in the book value of ABC's equity.

   (b) If the position is not a hedge of a predictable cash flow, the MTM change would be included in the calculation of ABC's current earnings.

CASE

Houston Marine Electronics

Foreign Exchange Valuation, International Parity Conditions, Forward FX Contracts, and Hedging FX Transaction Exposure

In early February of 2013, Stafford Johnson was looking out of his office window in Houston, contemplating the future of the Australian dollar and the recommendation he would soon make to his company's executive group. The company was Houston Marine Electronics, Inc. (HME), a producer of sonar equipment for private vessels. Johnson had been the company's Chief Financial Officer for nearly 10 years.

Background

HME was founded in 1979 by William "King" Kennedy. A veteran of the U.S. Navy, Kennedy had an extensive background in sonar technology. HME had been acquired in 2006 by Adventure and Recreation Technologies, Inc. (ART), a Nasdaq company, which had existing businesses in diving gear and watercraft, mainly canoes and kayaks. ART had promised Kennedy that he could continue as the CEO of HME, and that he could run the company without interference from ART's corporate headquarters in Boise, Idaho.

In recent years, HME continued to be one of the industry leaders in innovation, and was presently manufacturing two types of the new "360 sonar technology" products. One was the STE-19 model, nicknamed the "bird," which is a smaller piece of equipment for sport fishing boats and which retailed for $2,500. The other was the STX-27 model, called the "beast," which was designed for commercial fishing boats and luxury yachts and retailed for $10,000. In 2012, HME produced and sold 30,000 units of the "bird," for $75 million in revenues, and 2,500 units of the "beast," for $25 million in revenues. In 2012, HME contributed $100 million of ART's $300 million in revenues. Production of the "bird" units was shared equally by three plants, in Houston, Florida, and California, whereas the "beast" was produced solely in the Houston plant.

Executive Meeting

HME's top executives had met earlier in the week to discuss a new business development. Joining Kennedy and Johnson at the meeting were HME's Head of Sales, Stephen Magee; Chief Operations Officer, Betty Simkins; and Corporate Controller, Reilly White. By December 2012, Magee had developed a "live" sales lead with Chris Malone, the manager of onboard electronics systems for the giant Australian builder of luxury ships, Gold Coast Ships. Gold Coast had just launched its 5000th ship in 30 years of shipbuilding. Malone had bought a few units of the "beast" to check out the product and HME. Malone liked the product and HME's on-time delivery. He wanted to expand HME's role in Gold Coast's component supply chain.

Magee reported to the executive group that Gold Coast was proposing to buy 250 units of the "beast" in 2013 and 250 more in 2014, and had made a verbal offer of A$10,000 per unit, including shipping. Payments for 250 units, A$ 2.50 million, would be made annually at the end of each of the next two years. If completed, the deal would be the largest sale of Magee's career, and he was pushing the executive group for "yes."

Kennedy turned to the COO, Betty Simkins. "Betty, do we have the capacity to produce 250 more "beasts" per year?" Simkins said that it could be done, but that it would be costly. The Houston plant was at full capacity. He thought some of the Houston "bird" production could be shifted out to the Florida and California plants, and the Houston plant could then be restructured to increase "beast" production by the necessary 10%. However, she estimated that this change would result in incrementally higher variable production costs. Allocating the incremental production costs to the additional "beasts," and including shipping, the units produced for Gold Coast would have a variable cost of $8,000 per unit, about $500 per unit higher than for the "beasts" that were currently being produced. Kennedy wondered how ART's corporate group would react to the lower margin, but he knew it was his call to make. He thought the sale could open a large market for HME in Australia.

Kennedy next spoke to the CFO, Johnson. "Staff, what about the pricing in Australian dollars? Can we handle that?" Johnson said that it would be helpful if Magee could negotiate an agreement with Malone to share the foreign exchange risk, which might be possible particularly if Malone thought the Australian dollar would appreciate against the U.S. dollar over the next two years. Magee said he would check into that idea. Johnson added that even if Magee was successful, HME would still face some FX risk. He said he wanted a few days to further research the issue, and that he would report back at the next meeting, scheduled for later in the week.

Research

Johnson, who had a strong education in finance from the University of Texas, found the following information. The spot FX rate was currently around 1.04 $/A$ but was volatile. After reaching about 0.96 $/A$ in May of 2008, the currency had plummeted to about 0.65 $/A$ in January of 2009, was back up to 0.93 $/A$ in January 2010, and then traded between 0.85 $/A$ and 1.10 $/A$ until the present time.

Then Johnson studied the intrinsic value of the FX rate. First he found on the web the latest *Economist* magazine Big Mac Index, dated January 31, 2013. He saw that the Australian dollar was said to be overvalued by 12.2%, based on Big Mac prices. He computed a fair value for the FX rate based on the Big Mac purchasing power parity. Johnson also noted that the *Economist*'s Big Mac analysis contained an "adjusted index," which adjusts the FX valuation for country wealth by using the "line of best fit" between Big Mac prices and gross domestic product (GDP) per person. Here he noted that the Australian dollar was said to be undervalued by 14.6%. He computed the fair value of the spot FX rate using the adjusted Big Mac Index.

Johnson next searched the web for economists' forecasts for the FX rate. In one article, dated January 16, 2013, Johnson read that the

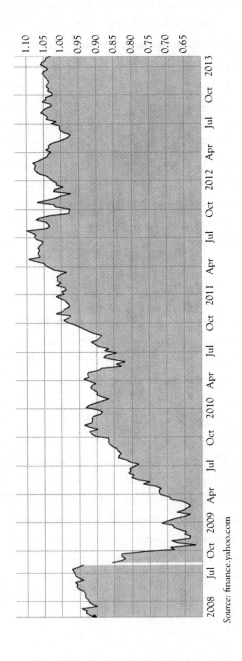

Source: finance.yahoo.com

Commonwealth Bank of Australia (CBA) was forecasting the FX rate to be 1.08 $/A$ at the end of 2013. He read that CBA's head of currency strategy expected improvement in the world economy in the year ahead, and said that strong commodity prices and an expectation the U.S. Federal Reserve will keep in place open-ended "quantitative easing" are further reasons to expect a higher Australian dollar. Johnson understood that quantitative easing involves keeping interest rates low. He knew he needed to be able to explain why the Australian dollar would probably drop in response to an increase in U.S. dollar interest rates or a decrease in Australian dollar interest rates.

Johnson next observed that the one-year interbank interest rates were 0.65% for the U.S. dollar and 3.29% for the Australian dollar. Based on the CBA forecast and the traditional uncovered interest rate parity (UIRP) condition, he calculated another estimate of the intrinsic value of the FX rate, which economists regard as an estimate of the short-run equilibrium FX rate. Given the actual spot FX rate of 1.04 $/A$, he calculated that the Australian dollar was undervalued by about 6.2%.

Johnson next called HME's bank for some retail forward FX quotes and retail interest rate quotes. He was told that HME could sell Australian dollars one-year forward at 1.012 $/A$ and two-years forward at 0.984 $/A$. The bank also told him that HME could borrow Australian dollars for one or two years at 3.50% and deposit U.S. dollars for one or two years at 0.50%. He computed the one-year and two-year synthetic forward FX rates at which he could put on a money market hedge.

Johnson began to weigh the pros and cons of hedging HME's potential FX transaction exposure to the Australian dollar. He called the controller, Reilly White, and asked him what he knew about the accounting implications of hedging with actual forward contracts and with money market hedges. Johnson asked White to prepare a slide and to be prepared to respond to questions on this issue at the upcoming meeting.

Presentation Preparation

Johnson began to prepare his presentation slides. On the first slide, he showed the chart for the historical movement of the $/A$ FX rate. He noted the current spot FX rate of 1.04 $/A$, the five-year low in January

2009 low of 0.65 $/A$ and the post-January 2010 low of 0.85 $/A$. He also knew that he had to be prepared to answer why the Australian dollar had dropped so far so fast in 2008, including the carry trade issues. He would likely be asked for his judgment on whether a drop like that could occur again in the next two years.

Slide 2 showed three "what if" estimates of the annual contribution (revenue minus variable production costs) of the sale to Gold Coast. The first estimate was based on today's spot FX rate of 1.04 $/A$. Next, to show the risk and its implications, he showed the annual contribution if the Australian dollar were to depreciate to the 0.85 $/A$ level. Finally, he showed the result at 0.65 $/A$. Johnson also showed three "what if" contribution estimates for the same FX rates, but under the assumption that Magee got Malone to agree to a "split the difference" pricing arrangement, where Gold Coast would pay the average of (a) A$ 10,000 per "beast," and (b) the payment that would be made if the "beast" price is fixed at today's equivalent in U.S. dollars, $10,400.

On Slide 3, Johnson showed the three estimates of intrinsic value of the FX rate: (a) the raw purchasing power parity (PPP) FX rate; (b) the adjusted PPP FX rate; and (c) the short-run UIRP FX rate. For the short-run estimate, he included how he made the calculation, and by what percentage the Australian dollar was presently over/undervalued. He also showed "what if" scenarios for how the intrinsic FX rate would be lower, and thus imply a drop in the Australian dollar, if either the U.S. dollar interest rate were to rise or the Australian dollar interest rate were to drop.

On Slide 4, Johnson showed the annual contribution (revenue minus variable production costs) of the sale to Gold Coast, based on the one-year and two-year actual forward FX rates. He assumed a fixed "beast" price of A$10,000 and that all payments would be received at the year end. He did the same using the synthetic one-year and two-year forward FX rates. He briefly explained the structure of a money market hedge and concluded whether actual forward FX contracts or money market hedges were better, given the data for this situation.

Reilly White prepared Slide 5, showing the accounting implications of the two-year forward FX position after one year elapsed, assuming a fixed "beast" price of A$10,000, that the actual spot FX rate was 0.90 $/A$ at that time, and that the one-year interbank interest rates are the same as today, 0.65% for U.S. dollars and 3.29% for Australian dollars.

Finally, Johnson concluded with a recommendation on whether to hedge the FX transaction exposure or not.

The Meeting and Questions

When the executives met again to resume their discussion of the potential contract with Gold Coast, Johnson made his presentation. During the presentation, five questions arose:

1. During Slide 1, Kennedy asked Johnson the expected question on why the FX rate had dropped so much in 2008, and how likely a similar drop to occur in the next two years was.
2. During Slide 3, Magee asked Johnson to explain how the *Economist* determined the Australian dollar to be undervalued by 14.6%, based on the adjusted PPP approach.
3. During Slide 4, Kennedy asked Johnson to explain how the one-year forward contract worked if the spot FX rate were 0.85 $/A$ a year hence.
4. During Slide 4, Simkins asked how the money market hedge would work.
5. During Slide 4, Simkins said, "I read an article that the OECD estimates the Australian dollar is presently overvalued by 60%, much more than your numbers suggest. This estimate would strengthen the argument for hedging with forward contracts, and suggests that we "overhedge" to try to profit from the correction of the Aussie dollar." Johnson responded that overhedging "would be risky, and has some negative accounting implications as well, which I will let Reilly White explain shortly."

Case Solution

Students are expected to make Johnson's and White's presentations and respond to the five questions raised. The solution includes the presentation slides and answers to the questions at the second executive meeting.

Conclusion

There is really no correct answer on whether HME should hedge the FX transaction exposure or not. The pros and cons of hedging should be discussed. It seems likely that many businesses would hedge this risk. There may also be some managers who are willing to speculate, given some analysis that the short-run financial market estimate of the intrinsic FX value of the Australian dollar indicates that the Australian dollar may be a bit undervalued.

Notes

Chapter 3

1. An interesting study of violations of the law of one price for some internationally distributed retail goods (of the IKEA Company) is in Haskel and Wolf (2001).
2. For interesting views on the trade deficit, see Ohmae (1991) and Pakko (1999).
3. See Cumby (1996).
4. See Parsley and Wei (2007).

Chapter 4

1. In algebraic terms, after the year has elapsed, the new spot FX rate, given that APPP also holds *after* the goods price changes, should be $X_{P1}^{\$/£} = [P_0^\$(1 + p^\$)]/[P_0^£(1 + p^£)]$. Substitute from equation (3.2) the time-0 FX rate of $X_{P0}^{\$/£} = P_0^\$/P_0^£$, and we have that the new (time-1) spot FX rate should be $X_{P0}^{\$/£}[(1 + p^\$)/(1 + p^£)]$. Equation (4.1) follows.
2. For a fascinating account of the FX market and the Bretton Woods conference, especially the role played by Keynes, see Krieger (1992). Another interesting account of the Bretton Woods conference and of the evolution of global markets is in Millman (1995).
3. For further information about the evolution of the international monetary system, see Chapter 2 of Levich (2001).
4. See M. Pakko and P. Pollard (2003).

Chapter 5

1. These ideas are based on Dornbusch (1976). Another helpful discussion of the Dornbusch model ideas is in Solnik and McLeavy (2009), p. 67.
2. See Bansal and Dahlquist (2000).

Chapter 6

1. Rearrange equation (5.1) to get $E(X_N^{Sf/\$})/X_{U0}^{Sf/\$} = [(1 + r^{Sf})/(1 + r^\$)]^N$. Take the Nth root of both sides to get that $[E(X_N^{Sf/\$})/X_{U0}^{Sf/\$}]^{1/N} = (1 + r^{Sf})/(1 + r^\$)$.

The annualized expected rate of return, $E(x_N^{S/\$})$, is equal to $[E(X_N^{S/\$})$ $/X_{U0}^{S/\$}]^{1/N} - 1$. So $1 + E^*(x_N^{S/\$}) = (1 + r^{S/})/(1 + r^{\$})$. This relationship is shown as a linear approximation in equation (6.1).

2. Siegel's paradox was introduced in Siegel (1975).

3. See Solnik (1993).

4. To derive equation (6.4), note that rearranged versions of the RPPP and UIRP conditions are $X_{P0}^{¥/\$} = E(X_N^{¥/\$})/[(1 + p^{¥})/(1 + p^{\$})]^N$ and $X_{U0}^{¥/\$} = E(X_N^{¥/\$})/[(1 + r^{¥})/(1 + r^{\$})]^N$. From these two expressions we have that $X_{U0}^{¥/\$}/X_{P0}^{¥/\$} = [(1 + r^{\$})/(1 + r^{¥})]^N/[(1 + p^{\$})/(1 + p^{¥})]^N$. Using equation (6.3b), we get equation (6.4).

Chapter 7

1. This scenario is from Jacque and Hawawini (1993).

Chapter 8

1. See Lipson (2008).

2. For a discussion of the issues in selective hedging and a survey of the practice in German firms, see Glaum (2002).

References

Bansal, R., & Dahlquist, M. (2000). The forward premium puzzle: Different tales from developed and emerging economies. *Journal of International Economics 51*(1), 115–144.

Click, R. (1996). Contrarian McParity. *Economics Letters 53*(2), 209–212.

Cumby, R. (1996). *Forecasting exchange rates and relative prices with the hamburger standard: Is what you want what you ret with McParity?* Retrieved January 1, 2006, from National Bureau of Economic Research site: http://www.nber.org/papers/w5675.pdf

Dornbusch, R. (1976). Expectations and exchange rate dynamics. *Journal of Political Economy 84*(6), 1161–1176.

Glaum, M. (2002). The determinants of selective exchange rate risk management-evidence from German non-financial corporations. *Journal of Applied Corporate Finance 14*(4), 108–121.

Haskel, J., & Wolf, H. (2001). The law of one price: A case study. *Scandinavian Journal of Economics 103*(4), 545–558.

Jacque, L., & Hawawini, G. (1993). Myths and realities of the global capital market: Lessons for managers. *Journal of Applied Corporate Finance 6*(3), 81–90.

Krieger, A. (1992). *The Money Bazaar.* New York, NY: Times Books.

Levich, R. (2001). *International Financial Markets* (2nd ed.). New York, NY: McGraw-Hill Irwin.

Lipson, M. (2008). *Baker Adhesives.* Darden Case No UVA-F-1516.

Millman, G. (1995), *The Vandal's Crown.* New York, NY: The Free Press.

Ohmae, K. (1991). Lies, damned lies, and statistics: Why the trade deficit doesn't matter in a borderless world. *Journal of Applied Corporate Finance 3*(4), 98–106.

Pakko, M. (1999) The U.S. trade deficit and the 'new economy'. *Review of the Federal Reserve Bank of St. Louis 81*(5), 11–19.

Pakko, M., & Pollard, P. (2003), Burgernomics: A Big Mac™ guide to purchasing power parity. *The Federal Reserve Bank of St. Louis 85*(6), 9–28.

Parsley, D., & Wei, S. (2007). A prism into the PPP puzzles: The micro-foundations of Big Mac real exchange rates. *Economic Journal 117*(523), 1336–1356.

Siegel, J. (1975). Risk, interest rates, and the forward exchange. *Quarterly Journal of Economics 89*(1), 173–175.

Solnik, B. (1993). Currency hedging and Siegel's paradox: On Black's universal hedging rule. *Review of International Economics 1*(2), 180–187.

Solnik, B., & McLeavy, D. (2009). *Global Investments* (6th ed.). Boston, MA: Pearson/Prentice-Hall.

Index